ENHANCING REGIONAL HEALTH COOPERATION UNDER CAREC 2030

A SCOPING STUDY

JULY 2021

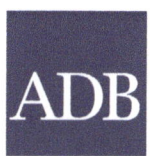

CONTENTS

TABLES, FIGURES, AND BOXES

TABLES

FIGURES

BOXES

FOREWORD

The coronavirus disease (COVID-19) pandemic has been a reminder to the global community that viruses do not stop at national borders. Cooperation between countries has once again proved to be a necessity in addressing regional health threats and safeguarding population health. Cooperation in health can also help find solutions for other challenges, such as addressing noncommunicable diseases (NCDs), upgrading skills of health care workers, protecting health of migrant workers, and providing quality health services to border communities.

The Central Asia Regional Economic Cooperation (CAREC) Program is a partnership of 11 countries, supported by the Asian Development Bank (ADB) and other development partners, working together to promote development through cooperation, leading to accelerated growth and poverty reduction. The CAREC 2030 strategy, endorsed at the 16th CAREC Ministerial Conference in October 2017, has expanded cooperation into new areas—including human development to better address the region's development needs and help its member countries achieve the 2030 Global Development Agenda. Health cooperation has been identified as a new priority area as part of the human development cluster under the CAREC 2030 strategy. It supports CAREC countries in addressing pandemic risks and control of communicable diseases, as well as in addressing NCDs.

This scoping study is a first step toward enhancing regional health cooperation in the CAREC region. It reviews the health sector progress and challenges and explores the potential role of CAREC in promoting regional cooperation for improved health outcomes in the region. The study reveals the extent of the burden of NCDs and communicable diseases in the CAREC region, and related strengths and weaknesses of health systems. It identifies the following strategic areas in advancing regional health cooperation: (i) strengthening regional health security; (ii) developing health systems through regional cooperation; and (iii) improving health services for migrants, mobile populations, and border communities. Given the COVID-19 pandemic, initial regional cooperation activities may focus on strengthening regional preparedness and resilience to ongoing and emerging infectious diseases. The study proposes the establishment of a working group for health comprising of relevant officials from CAREC countries, and the formulation of regional health strategy leading to 2030, to provide institutional support for health sector cooperation.

ADB would like to thank the active engagement and commitment of member countries to the process of advancing regional health cooperation. The scoping study was presented and discussed with CAREC countries and development partners at a virtual regional workshop on 15 October 2020. The study was then finalized, incorporating comments and suggestions from the CAREC countries. This study forms the basis of preparing a regional health strategy that is planned to be tabled for endorsement of CAREC Ministers in November 2021.

ADB, as a close partner of CAREC, looks forward to supporting this process and engaging with CAREC countries and development partners in jointly promoting and advancing regional health cooperation.

Yevgeniy Zhukov
Director General
Central and West Asia Department
Asian Development Bank

ACKNOWLEDGMENTS

This study was undertaken on behalf of the CAREC Secretariat of ADB. The team would like to thank Rie Hiraoka, director, Social Sector Division; and Safdar Parvez, director, Regional Cooperation and Operations Coordination Division, Central and West Asia Department, for the overall guidance.

The CAREC Secretariat at ADB administered and managed the production of this scoping study. The Secretariat team supporting CAREC health work includes Saad Paracha, senior regional cooperation specialist and CAREC unit head; Xinglan Hu, principal regional cooperation specialist; Rouselle Lavado, senior health specialist; Kirthi Ramesh, social sector specialist; Dorothea Lazaro, regional cooperation specialist; Irene de Roma, programs officer; Maria Cecilia Sison, operations assistant; and Gladys Ann R. Maravilla, operations assistant. Patricia Georgina Gonzales and Ammar Aftab, ADB consultants, provided data research. Reviews, inputs and feedback were provided by Eduardo Banzon, principal health specialist; Najibullah Habib, health specialist; Hiddo Huitzing, health specialist; Susann Roth, advisor and chief; Azusa Sato, health specialist; Cebele Wong, young professional; and Guoliang Wu, principal results management specialist.

The team expresses its appreciation to the regional cooperation coordinators and national focal points' advisors of all CAREC countries for the assistance extended in organizing the virtual regional consultation workshop. The team would also like to extend its profound gratitude to all participants of the health workshop for their valuable inputs, feedback, and contributions.

The team would further like to express their gratitude to experts and colleagues at the Global Fund (Alexey Bobrik, Michael Borowitz, Valeria Grishechkina, Corina Maxim, and Tatiana Vinichenko), Gavi, the Vaccine Alliance (Nilgun Aydogan, Santiago Cornejo, Jamilya Sherova, and Joanna Wisniewska), Project HOPE, Project ECHO (Bruce Baird Struminger), National Institute of Public Health in Mexico (Pedro Saturno Hernandez), UNICEF (Joan Howe and Artashes Mirzoyan), World Health Organization (WHO) (Dorit Nitzan), Institute for Health Metrics and Evaluation (Mohsen Naghavi and Sofia B. Redford), and Alan Lopez (University of Melbourne) who have been consulted during the preparation of this study and provided meaningful insights and suggestions.

The principal author of this study is Mariya Khatiwada-Savchuk. The contributions of all CAREC member countries and of WHO are acknowledged. Vincent De Wit provided peer review and additional inputs.

ABBREVIATIONS

ABEC	–	Almaty–Bishkek economic corridor
ADB	–	Asian Development Bank
AMR	–	antimicrobial resistance
ASEAN	–	Association of Southeast Asian Nations
CAREC	–	Central Asia Regional Economic Cooperation
CDC	–	Centers for Disease Control and Prevention
CID	–	chronic infectious disease
CIS	–	Commonwealth of Independent States
CPEC	–	China–Pakistan economic corridor
CVD	–	cardiovascular disease
COVID-19	–	coronavirus disease
EAEU	–	Eurasian Economic Union
EIDs	–	emerging infectious diseases
EIDSS	–	electronic integrated diseases surveillance system
e-SPAR	–	electronic state parties' self-assessment annual reporting
FELTP	–	field epidemiology and laboratory training program
GAVI	–	Gavi, the Vaccine Alliance
GDP	–	gross domestic product
GDDRC	–	Global Disease Detection Regional Center
GHSA	–	global health security agenda
GMS	–	Greater Mekong Subregion
HAI	–	hospital-acquired infections
HCV	–	hepatitis C virus
HTA	–	health technology assessment
HRH	–	human resources for health
ICT	–	information and communication technology
IFC	–	International Finance Corporation
IHR	–	International Health Regulations
ILO	–	International Labour Organization
IOM	–	International Organization for Migration
IMF	–	International Monetary Fund
JEE	–	joint external evaluation
JPA	–	joint procurement agreement
LMIC	–	lower middle-income country
MDR	–	multidrug-resistant
MERCOSUR	–	Mercado Común del Sur (Southern Common Market)
MERS	–	Middle East respiratory syndrome
MHIS	–	migrant health insurance scheme, Thailand
MIC	–	middle-income country

NCD	–	noncommunicable disease
OECD	–	Organisation for Economic Co-operation and Development
OECS	–	Organisation of Eastern Caribbean States
PHC	–	primary health care
PPP	–	purchasing power parity
PRC	–	People's Republic of China
RCI	–	regional cooperation and integration
RHC	–	regional health cooperation
RHS	–	regional health security
SARS	–	severe acute respiratory syndrome
SDG	–	Sustainable Development Goal
SPS	–	sanitary and phytosanitary
SSS	–	social security scheme, Thailand
SWOT	–	strengths, weaknesses, opportunities, threats
TAD	–	transboundary animal diseases
TB	–	tuberculosis
UHC	–	universal health coverage
UNICEF	–	United Nations Children's Fund
WHO	–	World Health Organization

EXECUTIVE SUMMARY

The Central Asia Regional Economic Cooperation (CAREC) Program is a partnership between development partners and member countries working together to promote development through cooperation, leading to accelerated economic growth and poverty reduction. The CAREC 2030 strategy seeks to expand economic cooperation in Central Asia by connecting people, policies, and projects toward shared and sustainable development. Promoting regional cooperation in the health sector is an operational priority under CAREC 2030.

While most of the CAREC countries have substantially reduced their poverty rates through economic liberalization, investments, and improvement of social services, poverty rate remains high in CAREC's fragile states. Growing socioeconomic ties have propelled the region's development; however, countries are facing new health sector challenges and the openness that enables increased movement of people and goods across borders has also facilitated the spread of infectious diseases, particularly the coronavirus disease (COVID-19). CAREC countries recognize the significance of regional health cooperation in managing regional health risks and supporting national health system development. Regional health cooperation provides an opportunity for countries to jointly strengthen health systems performance and financing, and to achieve better health outcomes.

This scoping study evaluates the potential of CAREC as a regional platform for promoting regional health cooperation, to mitigate regional health risks and build resilient national health systems. It reveals the challenges in regional health security; health systems development; and health care for migrants, mobile populations, and border communities. Based on a strengths, weaknesses, opportunities, and threats (SWOT) analysis, lessons and opportunities for regional cooperation have been identified.

Regional Health Challenges and Health Systems Development

CAREC countries are at various stages in their demographic and epidemiological transitions with declining mortality and morbidity from infectious diseases and an increasing mortality and morbidity from noncommunicable diseases (NCDs). While the overall burden of diseases in the CAREC region is dominated by NCDs, continual financing is required to control acute and chronic infectious diseases. There is also a persistent threat from emerging infectious diseases (EIDs), such as COVID-19, that can move across continents within a few months. Some CAREC countries are exposed to outbreaks of other communicable diseases, such as malaria, dengue, and Japanese encephalitis, that may spread regionally. Chronic infectious diseases such as HIV/AIDS, tuberculosis, and viral hepatitis B and C also have regional impact and continue to pose a heavy burden in CAREC countries.

The CAREC region is especially prone to outbreaks and epidemics due to its increasing connectivity, population mobility, urban hubs, and livestock raising and trading. Increasing labor migration further contributes to an increased threat of pandemics. Labor migrants, particularly the unskilled and undocumented, are often in poor working and living conditions. They have limited access to social protection and health services, which may eventually lead to health issues, especially infectious diseases.

Most CAREC countries have almost universal access to health services but their quality, especially in rural areas, remains substandard due to workforce and other resource constraints. CAREC countries face challenges in human resources for health such as an aging workforce, inappropriate staff mix and recruitment policies, urban–rural maldistribution and retention issues, substandard quality of education, weak enforcement of standards and accreditation, poor absorption capacity, poor career structure, and substandard working environment. National health information systems in the CAREC region are often fragmented due to parallel disease surveillance systems; lack of integration of the private sector; and fragmentation between facilities at national, provincial, and local level. The quality, availability, and affordability of medicines are a major concern, particularly the trade in substandard and fake medicines, and related over-the-counter sale and incorrect use that contribute to the emergence of drug resistance. The CAREC region is also challenged with limited health financing to address the increasing burden of NCDs and achieve universal health coverage and the Sustainable Development Goals (SDGs).

Several regional organizations and groupings are engaging in health cooperation, some countries have signed bilateral agreements, and various subregional and cross-border initiatives on health cooperation exist. However, the CAREC region would benefit from an enhanced common strategic approach for improving regional health security in terms of mobilization of goodwill and resources, knowledge and information exchange, capacity building and technology transfer, and joint outbreak response. Preparedness, surveillance and response, hospital and laboratory upgrading, and human resource development need improvement at the national level.

Opportunities and Recommendations for Regional Health Cooperation

Regional and cross-border cooperation is driven by joint regional interests and benefits (direct and indirect). Successful regional cooperation depends on factors such as leadership, consensus among parties, technical capacity, and resources. Economic rationales for regional cooperation include (i) generating commitment, competition, and leverage; (ii) economies of scale to improve services and efficiency; (iii) knowledge and technology transfer for analysis, policy making, and capacity building; and (iv) provision of regional public goods and services with externalities that are particularly important in the health sector. Regional cooperation has four dimensions: (i) cultural and social, (ii) geographic and demographic, (iii) regulatory, and (iv) economic and technological. Each dimension includes one or more potential driving factors for cross-border health collaboration.

The study's scoping of the drivers and constraints of regional health cooperation and the SWOT analysis has yielded key lessons suggesting to (i) develop regional and cross-border cooperation step by step; (ii) ensure viable plans with assessments, buy-in from stakeholders, clear agreements, pilots, and sustainable funding, examine financing mechanisms and propose realistic programming; (iii) seek institutional partnerships such as between national communicable diseases control institutions or with third parties and where feasible, build on existing initiatives; (iv) facilitate with regional oversight, focal points, and a secretariat; (v) institutionalize and further strengthen regional health cooperation at national level as an essential part of the health sector structure, staff responsibilities, and budget; and (vi) assess the value addition of regional health initiatives vis-à-vis national-level solutions.

Three overall and interlinked objectives are identified as strategic areas for Regional Health Cooperation: (i) strengthening regional health security (RHS); (ii) supporting health systems development through regional cooperation; and (iii) improving health care for migrants, mobile populations, and border communities.

Strengthen regional health security. Strengthening RHS requires CAREC cooperation in addressing public health threats, such as COVID-19, and in better preparing countries for future public health threats. Several areas for cooperation in regional health security can be explored, such as regional surveillance (including modeling and forecasting) and strengthening the One Health approach particularly for food safety, the control of zoonoses, and combatting antibiotic resistance. CAREC's regional cooperation in health would add value to ongoing COVID-19 response efforts to build resilient health systems and enhance health security capabilities. CAREC also needs to conduct further in-depth assessments to scope selected regional mechanisms, as well as joint capacity building and simulation exercises that can strengthen regional health security based on lessons from the COVID-19 pandemic.

Support health systems development through regional cooperation. To address national and regional health threats, focus can be on building health systems capacities by improving human resources for health, health information systems, and access to medicines and technology. Improving human resources for health may start with assessing health workforce requirements to support national health strategies toward achieving universal health coverage and the SDGs, as well as the potential for regional collaboration. Improving health information systems can focus on integrating the fragmented health information systems at national level, facilitating harmonization of eHealth standards at regional level, and exploring how innovative digital health can strengthen regional health cooperation. To increase access to medicines and technology, CAREC countries may jointly facilitate pharmaceutical manufacturing in the region through transfer of technologies and pool the procurement of medicines in the region for economies of scale.

Improve health care for migrants, mobile populations, and border communities. Regional cooperation in this area may include improving data collection and purposeful sharing of information on access to health care for migrants, improving information at pre-departure stages, updating and harmonizing provisions for access under bilateral agreements, and introducing fully pledged migrant health insurance schemes. CAREC cooperation in regional health insurance scheme may require a series of investment projects involving subgroups of countries with a strong common goal of improving access to health care for migrants. There is potential to further assess cross-border health services along the CAREC economic corridors and further scope feasibility of cross-border specialty care. Joint regional strategies could support protecting the most vulnerable residing in border areas from disease outbreaks and improve their access to health services.

Since health is a new sector under the CAREC 2030 strategy, cooperation can be undertaken in a phased approach, starting with initial areas (such as dialogue and knowledge sharing), then gradually expanding into more complex areas (such as harmonization of standards). Containing COVID-19 and distilling lessons learned will be a priority for cooperation in the short term.

Given its joint legacy, geographic proximity, and existing cross-border cooperation, the CAREC region has strong foundations for regional health cooperation. Tackling regional health threats and related health services and health systems development requires regional actions, particularly functional regional mechanisms for policy dialogue and information sharing on health sector issues. Through the CAREC platform, countries can jointly address emerging and chronic infectious diseases and NCDs by improving regional health security; developing responsive and resilient health systems; and improving health services for migrants, mobile populations, and border communities.

The scoping study was shared, presented, and discussed with representatives of governments and development partners. Representatives of CAREC member countries agreed to establish a Working Group on Health to discuss CAREC's potential role and value addition in the health sector, formulate scope of engagement and priorities through the development of a CAREC health strategy toward 2030, and set up institutional arrangements for regional health cooperation.

2021

Priority in
SHORT TERM

Start with
EASIER ARE

Containing
COVID-19

Distilling
lessons learned

Assessments, knowledge e
coordination, joint capac
and planni

1 Streng
health

Reality Check

Regional Health Challenges

NCD

Noncommunicable diseases (NCD) form the largest part of the overall burden of disease in the region.

Emerging infectious and other communicable diseases are declining but remain a threat

Continual financing required to control acute and chronic infectious diseases.

Emerging infectious diseases, such as COVID-19, pose persistent threat

Epidemics and pandemics

The CAREC region is especially prone to outbreaks due to increasing connectivity, population mobility, urban hubs, and livestock raising and trading

Labor migrants are often in poor working and living conditions with limited access to social protection and health services.

Malaria, dengue, and Japanese encephalitis

Some CAREC countries are exposed to outbreaks of other communicable diseases

Reality Check

Health System Development

The quality of health services, especially in rural areas, remains substandard.

Challenges in the health workforce
- Aging workforce
- Staff mix and recruitment
- Urban–rural maldistribution
- Education
- Enforcement of standards and accreditation

Fragmented national health information systems
- Parallel surveillance systems
- Lack of integration of the private sector
- Fragmentation between facilities at national, provincial, and local level

The quality, availability, and affordability of medicines
- Substandard and falsified medicines
- Over-the-counter sale and incorrect use of antibiotics resulting in increasing antimicrobial resistance

CAREC = Central Asia Regional Economic Cooperation Program, COVID-19 = coronavirus disease.

CAREC 2030: ENHANCING REGIONAL HEALTH COOPERATION

Harmonization of standards, setting up
regional mechanisms, and cross-border solutions

CAREC 2030

, dialogue,
opment,

regional
rity

Regional surveillance and rapid response
One Health approach
Regional health security infrastructure
International Health Regulations
Combatting antimicrobial resistance

ealth
eats

dd value to ongoing COVID-19 response efforts

3 Strategic areas for Regional Health Cooperation

Support health systems development through regional cooperation

• Assessing health workforce requirements to support national health strategies

nan resources
for health

Access to medicines and technology

• Advance transfer of technologies to facilitate pharmaceutical manufacturing in the region
• Advance regulatory coordination and reliance policies
• Explore joint procurement

• Leveraging innovative digital solutions to advance regional health cooperation
• Harmonization of eHealth standards and advancing interoperability

nformation systems

3 Improve health care for migrants, mobile populations, and border communities

• Assessing current state of portability of health care benefits and liabilities across borders
• Develop joint strategies to improve access to health services for most vulnerable in border areas
• Further assess cross-border health services along the CAREC economic corridors

• Improving information at pre-departure stages
• Support regional collaboration in access and financing of health services for migrants
• Introducing fully pledged migrant health insurance schemes

1

INTRODUCTION

1.1 Central Asia in Transition

1. Central Asia, including the Transcaucasian region, is strategically located along the historic silk roads between East Asia and Europe, a distinct ecological zone wedged in between the Middle East and North and South Asia.[1] The land and people of Central Asia have been shaped by civilizations for thousands of years. They are tied geographically, socially and commercially, with a shared history and common legacy, but differ in their political and economic development context, and cultural and ethnic composition. Countries that were part of the former Soviet Union have inherited different political and public services structures than other countries and have undertaken different reforms.

2. Central Asia has experienced a very rapid but mixed economic development over the past 2 decades. In this period, per capita income in Kazakhstan and Turkmenistan has increased about tenfold. Afghanistan, the Kyrgyz Republic, and Tajikistan have seen less economic growth, while Azerbaijan, Georgia, Mongolia, Pakistan, the People's Republic of China (PRC), and Uzbekistan have shown substantial economic growth.[2] Several of these countries have a natural resource-based economy, which makes them highly dependent on price movements in the global market. The less endowed countries are also highly dependent on migrant labor, especially to the Russian Federation, and on foreign investments and assistance, making these countries more vulnerable to economic crisis.

3. Countries in Central Asia have substantially reduced their poverty rates through economic liberalization, investments, and improvement of social services. However, poverty rate remains high in Afghanistan at 54.5% and Tajikistan at 26.3%, which are both below the national poverty line.[3] Countries in Central Asia vary significantly in terms of state fragility and social safety nets to protect their citizens. The 2018 United Nations human development index of these countries ranged from 0.496 for Afghanistan to 0.817 for Kazakhstan, while the inequality adjusted human development index ranged from 0.386 for Pakistan to 0.759 for Kazakhstan.[4] Gender equity continues to be a major challenge in the region. The gender development index is low at 0.663 for Afghanistan and 0.747 for Pakistan.

1.2 The CAREC 2030 Strategy

4. With stewardship of the Asian Development Bank (ADB), the Central Asia Regional Economic Cooperation (CAREC) Program was established in 2001 to encourage economic cooperation among countries in Central Asia and nearby parts of Transcaucasia, South Asia, and East Asia. Its current 11 member countries and development partners are working together to promote development through regional cooperation, leading to accelerated economic growth and poverty reduction.[5] Initial CAREC member countries include Afghanistan,

---

[1] P. Frankopan. 2015. *The Silk Roads: A New History of the World*. London: Bloomsbury Publishing.

[2] World Bank. GDP per capita (current US$) – Tajikistan, Uzbekistan, Kyrgyz Republic, Turkmenistan, Kazakhstan (accessed 3 August 2020). https://data.worldbank.org/indicator/NY.GDP.PCAP.CD?locations=TJ-UZ-KG-TM-KZ.

[3] World Bank. Poverty headcount ratio at national poverty lines (% of population) – Afghanistan, Tajikistan (accessed 12 December 2020). https://data.worldbank.org/indicator/SI.POV.NAHC?locations=TJ-AF.

[4] UNDP. Human Development Reports. Global Human Development Indicators (accessed 12 December 2020). http://hdr.undp.org/en/countries/profiles.

Azerbaijan, Kazakhstan, the Kyrgyz Republic, Mongolia, the PRC (Xinjiang Uygur Autonomous Region and Inner Mongolia Autonomous Region since 2008), Tajikistan, and Uzbekistan. Pakistan and Turkmenistan joined in 2010, and Georgia in 2016.

5. The CAREC 2030 strategy, endorsed at the 16th Ministerial Conference in October 2017, seeks to expand the horizons of economic cooperation in the region by connecting people, policies, and projects. The strategy supports regional cooperation and integration of CAREC member countries toward shared and sustainable development. The CAREC 2030 strategic framework has five operational clusters: (i) economic and financial stability; (ii) trade, tourism, and economic corridors; (iii) infrastructure and economic connectivity; (iv) agriculture and water; and (v) human development including health.[6] Information and communication technology (ICT) is a crosscutting priority of all CAREC operations. The operational cluster for human development envisages strengthening regional health cooperation (RHC) under the CAREC framework.

6. CAREC 2030 is strategically aligned with the international development agenda. All CAREC countries are signatories to the 2030 global development agenda, including the Sustainable Development Goals (SDGs) and the Paris Agreement reached at the 21st Conference of the Parties of United Nations Framework Convention on Climate Change (COP21). The United Nations and global finance institutions affirm that better health makes an important contribution to well-being, economic progress, and sustainable development. SDG 3 aims to "ensure healthy lives and promote well-being for all at all ages." Its centerpiece, universal health coverage (UHC), signifies that all people should have access to quality health services when in need, without facing financial hardship. SDG 3 is interwoven with nine other SDGs targeting health-related issues including poverty reduction (SDG 1), gender equality (SDG 5), and water and sanitation (SDG 6).

1.3 A Case for Regional Health Cooperation

7. The world has entered a new phase of international relations and global health diplomacy, amid growing national alliance with global aspirations, especially toward achieving SDGs and UHC. Countries around the world increasingly recognize their health interdependency with neighboring countries and the world. Interdependencies range from the spread of communicable diseases, or drug resistance, to factors that impact health outcomes and health systems such as water and food shortages, climate change, research and development of drugs and vaccines, lifestyle changes, or migration. These call for greater cooperation between states as well as cross-sector policies and collaboration.[7] Countries increasingly rely on the global community in addressing national health challenges. These interdependencies have been evident in the coronavirus disease (COVID-19) pandemic.

8. CAREC countries recognize that RHC is vital in managing regional health risks and supporting national health systems development.

---

[5]   ADB. 2012. *CAREC 2020: A Strategic Framework for the CAREC Program*. Manila.

[6]   ADB. 2017. *CAREC 2030: Connecting the Region for Shared and Sustainable Development*. Manila.

[7]   I. Kickbusch et al. 2007. Global Health Diplomacy: The Need for New Perspectives, Strategic Approaches and Skills in Global Health. *Bulletin of the World Health Organization*. 85 (3). March. pp. 161–244. 3. https://www.who.int/bulletin/volumes/85/3/06-039222/en/.

Regional cooperation in health is found in several national strategies and existing initiatives, particularly in cross-border control of diseases, preparing for pandemics, seeking common solutions for noncommunicable diseases (NCDs), and providing health services in border areas. There is scope to further promote regional cooperation in the health sector with CAREC as a regional platform.

9. CAREC countries also experience major national public health challenges. The population, health, and nutrition status of CAREC countries have improved dramatically along with socioeconomic development. However, with population aging in several countries and changing lifestyles, countries in the region are facing a triple burden of disease, specifically communicable diseases, NCDs, and accidents and injuries.[8]

10. RHC provides an opportunity for countries to jointly strengthen health systems performance and financing and achieve better health outcomes. The health sector is fast becoming one of the largest and most challenging sectors in terms of employment and financing, and is expected to experience a growing demand for high-quality medical services. This will put pressure on the limited human resources and financing, and widen the gap in primary health care (PHC). Central Asia was the birthplace of the PHC approach in 1978. This part of the health system will continue to require support.[9] While recognized as providing vital services, the public sector is often underfunded, and viewed as less efficient. On the other hand, the upcoming private health sector has been less regulated, resulting in poor value for money.

11. The COVID-19 pandemic amplifies the importance of building resilient national health systems and strengthening regional cooperation for health. It shows that, with increased global connectivity, a novel coronavirus of modest virulence can spread around the world within 6 months, and that local control measures can slow down but not stop outbreaks. It also demonstrates the limited preventive and curative surge capacity for emergencies in most countries, and the reliance on quick technical and financial assistance. Furthermore, it underlines the importance of the prevention and control of NCDs.[10]

12. Multiple international, regional, and local organizations are engaged in subregional and cross-border initiatives in health cooperation in the region, especially in infectious disease control of regional importance and currently COVID-19 (Appendix 5), but also in health services and other areas. Some countries have signed bilateral agreements on regional cooperation in health. At the same time, the CAREC region lacks a common strategic approach for improving regional health security, developing national health systems through regional cooperation, and improving access to health care for migrants and cross-border populations. It could benefit from a holistic regional approach that would support alignment among all CAREC member countries and provide a regional platform for dialogue and action. Regional cooperation is challenging and has to be firmly footed in mutual interest and trust, and add value beyond what national health systems can do. This scoping study explores this potential as a first step toward health cooperation in the CAREC region.

---

[8] While infectious diseases have declined, ongoing financing and efforts are required to keep these under control.

[9] In 2018, the Astana conference reconfirmed the strength of the PHC approach with more emphasis on multisector cooperation to achieve health for all by all, clearly recognizing the role all sectors play in health. World Health Organization (WHO). 2018. *The Astana Declaration of Primary Health Care*. Geneva.

[10] COVID-19 patients with comorbidities are more likely to have severe disease and subsequent mortality. R. Pal and S. K. Bhadada. 2020. COVID-19 and Non-Communicable Diseases. *Postgraduate Medical Journal*. 96. March. pp. 429–430.

13. The COVID-19 pandemic and its aftermath provide a unique opportunity to take stock of the health sector, initiate major actions to achieve the SDGs, and scope possibilities to deepen RHC. After the COVID-19 pandemic, governments and institutions should not relax their demonstrated support for the health sector but renew their commitments and efforts toward health for all. While CAREC countries have successfully harnessed cooperation for economic growth, they must now work together to tackle regional and national health threats. Given the pertinence of RHC, the CAREC Secretariat has conducted a scoping study to explore opportunities for RHC within the CAREC strategic framework.

1.4 The Scoping Study

14. The scoping study assesses the potential of CAREC as a regional platform for promoting RHC, so as to mitigate regional health risks and build resilient national health systems. The study aims to profile the health and health sector trends in the region; summarize the contributions of major stakeholders; identify strengths, weaknesses, opportunities, and threats (SWOT) for RHC; and provide recommendations of scope and implementation. The study is primarily a desk review with advice from institutional and country-based stakeholders. ADB will support additional assessments and consultations on the study's initial findings and recommendations with member countries and potential beneficiaries.

15. The study reviews the drivers and challenges of, and the rationale and opportunities for CAREC's RHC. Chapter 2 discusses the health trends and health systems development in the region. In Chapter 3, the study reflects on the lessons learned based on the drivers and constraints and SWOT analysis of regional health development and cooperation in CAREC. Chapter 3 also presents the opportunities for CAREC regional cooperation, drawing upon international experiences in specific areas. Chapter 4 provides recommendations covering policies, strategies, systems, and implementation arrangements.

2

HEALTH TRENDS AND SYSTEMS DEVELOPMENT IN THE CAREC REGION

2.1 Population, Health, and Nutrition Trends

16.   Life expectancies have increased across the region (Table 1). The average life expectancy in CAREC is above 70 years, with the highest at 76 years (PRC) and lowest at 64 years (Afghanistan). Women enjoy a longer life expectancy than men by about 5 years on average across the countries. Former Soviet Union republics that are in the upper middle-income countries (UMICs) group show lower life expectancies than the average for UMICs (75.5 years). Eastern Europe and Central Asia display a lower life expectancy than their Western neighbors. This is linked to higher perinatal and infant mortality; a high burden of NCDs among working-age males; and a higher burden of chronic infectious diseases (CIDs) including tuberculosis (TB), HIV, and hepatitis B and C.

Table 1: Life Expectancy and Fertility Indicators for CAREC Countries

Country/Region	Life Expectancy at Birth		Under-Five Mortality Rate (per 1,000 live births)		Total Fertility Rate (births per woman)	
	1990	2018	1990	2018	1990	2018
Afghanistan	50	64	175	63	7.5	4.5
Azerbaijan	65	73	95	22	2.7	1.7
China, People's Republic of	69	77	54	9	2.4	1.7
Georgia	70	74	48	10	2.2	2.1
Kazakhstan	68	73	53	10	2.7	2.8
Kyrgyz Republic	68	71	66	19	3.6	3.3
Mongolia	60	70	108	17	4.1	2.9
Pakistan	60	67	139	69	6.0	3.5
Tajikistan	63	71	105	35	5.2	3.6
Turkmenistan	63	68	84	42	4.3	2.8
Uzbekistan	66	72	72	18	4.1	2.4
Averages by regional and income grouping						
World	65	73	93	39	3.3	2.4
Europe, Central Asia	72	78	31	8	1.7	1.8
LIC	51	63	180	70	6.3	4.6
LMIC	59	68	122	51	4.2	2.8
UMIC	69	75	52	14	2.6	1.9

CAREC = Central Asia Regional Economic Cooperation, LIC = low income countries, LMIC = lower middle-income countries, UMIC = upper middle-income countries.

Source: World Bank. World Development Indicators. https://data.worldbank.org/indicator/SP.DYN.LE00.IN?locations=AF-AZ-CN-GE-KZ-KG-MN-PK-TJ-TM-UZ (accessed 12 December 2020).

17.   The positive health trends and the high proportion of population under age 14 in some CAREC countries point to favorable demographic perspectives with ample supply of young labor in the coming decades. Countries like Afghanistan, Pakistan, Tajikistan, and Uzbekistan have young and growing populations. This "population dividend" can benefit future economic development if managed well. Simultaneously, the share of elderly population is growing in CAREC countries. Georgia and the PRC already have a large share of people aged 65 and over (15% in Georgia and 11% in the PRC); and the trend shows that the population structure will continue to be more tilted toward aging (Appendix A1.2 Demographic Indicators).[11] Aging populations will add to the burden of NCDs, and put more strain on health systems and resources.

18.   CAREC countries are at various stages in their demographic and epidemiological transitions with declining mortality and morbidity from infectious diseases and an increasing mortality and morbidity from NCDs. Of the 10 CAREC countries, 5 report that NCDs constitute nearly or more than 85% of the total burden of disease (Figure 1, not including Turkmenistan).[12] Afghanistan and Pakistan are in the early stage of transition, with declining but high burden from infectious diseases and increasing burden from NCDs and accidents and injuries, resulting in a triple burden of disease faced by all CAREC countries.[13] It should be noted that, while in most CAREC countries, the burden of infectious diseases has declined substantially, all countries need to continue investing in prevention, control, and treatment efforts to sustain infectious diseases control. An overview of selected indicators is available in Appendix 1.

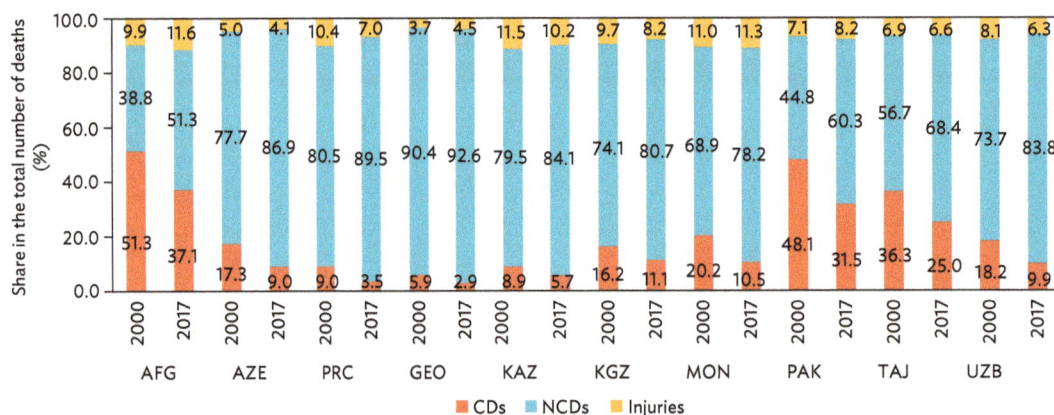

Figure 1: Distribution of Annual Mortality [Rate] by Causes in CAREC Region, 2000–2017

AFG = Afghanistan, AZE = Azerbaijan, CD = communicable disease, GEO = Georgia, KAZ = Kazakhstan, KGZ = Kyrgyz Republic, MON = Mongolia, NCD = noncommunicable disease, PAK = Pakistan, PRC = People's Republic of China, TAJ = Tajikistan, UZB = Uzbekistan.

Note: Data for Turkmenistan are not available.

Source: Institute for Health Metrics and Evaluation. 2018. *Global Burden of Disease Study Results, 2017*. Seattle, Washington. http://ghdx.healthdata.org/gbd-results-tool (accessed December 2019).

---

[11]   World Bank. World Development Indicators (WDI Tables). 2019. http://wdi.worldbank.org/table/2.1 (accessed 21 January 2019).

[12]   The main types of NCDs are cardiovascular diseases (like heart attacks and stroke), cancers, chronic respiratory diseases (such as chronic obstructive pulmonary disease and asthma), and diabetes.

[13]   WHO. 2018. *UHC and SDG Country Profile 2018: China*. Geneva.

2.2 Common Risk Factors Affecting Health in the Region

19.   Health outcomes are closely linked to the prevalence of risk factors and underlying determinants of health, some of which increasingly have a cross-border character and require cross-sector responses. Socioeconomic development (i.e., better education, roads, trade, productivity, and employment) has resulted in poverty reduction and gains in life expectancy and health in the CAREC region. Despite these gains, existing and emerging risk factors and underlying health determinants will continue to affect the populations' health status. These determinants include poverty rates, urbanization, labor migration, human-animal interaction, environmental pollution, as well as preventable and modifiable risk factors that particularly affect the burden of NCDs (e.g., unhealthy diet, physical inactivity, and substance abuse including tobacco and alcohol).[14] Table 2 summarizes several

Table 2: Health Risk Indicators in the CAREC Region

Indicators	AFG	AZE	PRC	GEO	KAZ	KGZ	MON	PAK	TAJ	TKM	UZB
Poverty %	54.5	6.0	0.6	19.5	4.3	20.1	28.4	24.3	26.3	...	14.1
Lower secondary education %[a]	55.3	84.7	99.5	113.9	117.9	71.1	106.5	49.5	96.2	80.1	94.7
Access to drinking water %[a]	67.1	91.4	92.8	98.4	95.6	87.5	83.3	91.5	81.2	98.8	97.8
Access to sanitation %[a]	43.4	92.5	84.8	90.0	97.9	96.5	58.5	59.9	97.0	98.7	100
Undernourishment %[a]	29.9	2.5	2.5	8.2	2.5	6.4	21.3	12.3	...	4.0	2.6
Male tobacco use %[b]	44.2[c]	39.0	47.7	54.2	42.2	52.5	49.1	33.6	14.7[d]	15.5[e]	23.3
Female tobacco use %[b]	5.4[c]	0.2	1.8	5.2	6.6	3.4	6.2	6.4	0.3[d]	0.6[e]	1.3
Male alcohol use liters[a]	0.4	7.5	10.9	13.6	7.9	10.8	12.8	0.6	5.6	8.4	4.5
Female alcohol use liters[a]	0.1	1.5	3.0	3.6	1.9	2.0	3.8	0.1	1.0	1.7	0.8
Air pollution deaths/100,000[b]	95.0	55.0	140.0	184.0	57.0	74.0	97.0	113.0	70.0	51.0	54.0
RTA deaths/100.000[b]	15.1	8.7	18.2	15.3	17.6	15.4	16.5	14.3	18.1	14.5	11.5.0

... = data not available, AFG=Afghanistan, AZE=Azerbaijan, CAREC = Central Asia Regional Economic Cooperation, GEO=Georgia, KAZ=Kazakhstan, KGZ=Kyrgyz Republic, MON=Mongolia, PAK=Pakistan, PRC=People's Republic of China, RTA=road traffic accidents; TAJ=Tajikistan, TKM=Turkmenistan, UZB=Uzbekistan.
Notes:
1. Poverty headcount ratio at national poverty lines (% of population), latest 2012–2019.
2. Lower secondary education completion rate % (of relevant age group), latest 2011-2019.
3. People using at least basic clean drinking water services and at least basic sanitation services, 2017.
4. Prevalence of undernourishment (% of population), 2018.
5. Tobacco use as a % of persons 15 years and above per year, 2018, except for AFG (15-45 years) 2015, TAJ 2016, TKM 2014.
6. Total alcohol consumption per capita, female and male (liters of pure alcohol, projected estimates, 15+ years of age), 2018.
7. Air pollution: crude death rate per 100,000 people per year due to combined household and ambient air pollution, 2016.
8. RTA deaths per 100,000 people per year, 2016.
[a] World Bank. World Bank Indicators. https://data.worldbank.org/indicator Accessed February 2021.
[b] United Nations. UN SDG database. https://unstats.un.org/sdgs/indicators/database/. Accessed February 2021. Except for tobacco use in AFG, TAJ, TKM.
[c] Afghanistan: Q. Alemi, C. Stempel, and S. Montgomery. 2020. Prevalence and Social Determinants of Tobacco Use in Afghanistan. *International Health.* 13 (1). pp. 3–12. https://academic.oup.com/inthealth/article/13/1/3/5821548;
[d] Tajikistan: H. Ismoilov. 2017. Results of the Adults on the Consumption of Tobacco Products. Statistical Agency under the President of the Republic of Tajikistan. Presentation during the Workshop on "Tobacco Questions for Surveys (TQS): Data Analysis and Dissemination." Ankara, Turkey. 16–17 August. https://www.sesric.org/imgs/news/1737-PRESENTATION-TQS-TAJIKISTAN-Hafizulloh-ISMOILOV-EN.pdf;
[e] Turkmenistan: World Health Organization Regional Office for Europe. 2017. *Tobacco Control Fact Sheet: Turkmenistan.* https://www.euro.who.int/__data/assets/pdf_file/0010/337438/Tobacco-Control-Fact-Sheet-Turkmenistan.pdf.
Source: Author.

[14] C. P. Benziger, G. A. Roth, and A. E. Moran. 2016. The Global Burden of Disease Study and the Preventable Burden of NCD. *Global Heart.* 8 December. 11 (4). pp. 393–397. doi: 10.1016/j.gheart.2016.10.024.

predisposing factors that affect the population's health status in CAREC countries. Other risk factors include gender, education, and water and sanitation coverage.

20.   Statistics show that cardiovascular risk factors, high rates of smoking, alcohol intake, elevated blood pressure, obesity, and diabetes are prevalent in the majority of CAREC countries, particularly in Georgia.[15] Over the past decade, most countries in the region have seen a decline in smoking prevalence.[16] However, they still have some of the highest numbers in the world.[17] Pakistan and the PRC also face significant

mortality attributed to indoor and ambient air pollution (Table 2).

21.   More efforts are required to reduce health risk factors through better prevention, preparedness, mitigation, and cross-sector approaches. The importance of the prevention and control of diseases in improving health indicators is often underappreciated. As populations live longer and better, improvement of health indicators will increasingly depend on a healthy environment and lifestyle, and on access to advanced medical services.

2.3 Health Challenges of Regional Importance

Emerging Infectious Diseases

22.   While the overall burden of diseases in the CAREC region is dominated by NCDs, continual financing is required to control acute and chronic infectious diseases. There is also a persistent threat from emerging infectious diseases (EIDs) that can move across and jump between countries and continents rapidly. The CAREC region is especially prone to outbreaks and epidemics due to its increasing connectivity, population mobility, urban hubs, and livestock raising and trading. In 2016, Kazakhstan airports handled 12.2 million passengers compared to about 4 billion flights globally.[18] Tourist arrivals in the region were estimated at about 20 million in 2018, and expected to grow sharply.[19] Even in smaller CAREC countries, thousands of

people and truckloads of livestock cross borders each day. It is evident that it is not possible to prevent infections from entering a country, hence better disaster risk reduction (prevention, preparedness, and mitigation) and resilience building are required.

23.   Most of the EIDs and endemic infectious diseases are of zoonotic origin. Viral infections like avian influenza and corona may be passed on from high metabolism animals like birds and bats through intermediate mammalian hosts to humans. Zoonotic diseases may endanger public health through human–animal interface, or human–to–human transmission. More than three-fifths of all diseases that affect humans are considered to be zoonotic in nature and three-quarters of all emerging infectious diseases

---

[15]   S. Russell. 2019. The Burden of Non-Communicable Diseases and Their Related Risk Factors in the Country of Georgia, 2015. *BMC Public Health*. 19 (479). 10 May. doi: 10.1186/s12889-019-6785-2.

[16]   Data not available for Afghanistan, Tajikistan, and Turkmenistan.

[17]   WHO. World Health Organization, Global Health Observatory Data Repository. https://www.who.int/data/gho/data/indicators/indicator-details/GHO/gho-tobacco-control-monitor-current-tobaccouse-tobaccosmoking-cigarrettesmoking-agestd-tobagestdcurr (accessed May 2020).

[18]   ADB. 2018. *Aviation and the Role of CAREC: A Scoping Study*. Manila.

[19]   ADB. 2019. *Promoting Regional Tourism Cooperation under CAREC 2030*. Manila. This number excludes tourism arrivals in Afghanistan, the PRC Autonomous Regions of Inner Mongolia and Xinjiang Uygur, and Turkmenistan.

are of animal origin, including COVID-19.[20] Zoonotic diseases are often caused by novel viruses that can only be detected once an outbreak occurs. Rabies, anthrax, brucellosis, leishmaniasis, and the Crimean-Congo hemorrhagic fever are long established zoonotic diseases of public health concern in Pakistan.[21]

24.   Livestock production is an important contributor to the economies of most CAREC countries and an important part of cross-border trade. As nations grow more prosperous, there is a growing demand for meat as a source of protein in diets. This leads to increased meat production, sometimes with poor biosafety standards and misuse of hormones and medicines. The large animal livestock population, poor biosafety standards, and substandard food hygiene contribute to the spread of new germs with potential drug resistance. Consequently, transboundary animal diseases (TADs) are an important veterinary and public health priority. These diseases can seriously disrupt trade of animal products, causing major losses in national export income in significant livestock-producing countries (e.g., Kazakhstan, Mongolia), as well as threaten food security through serious loss of animal protein. Unfortunately, there are few available vaccines and treatments for these diseases. Pursuing the One Health approach, a coordinated, multidisciplinary and cross-sectoral effort to address risks stemming from the animal–human–ecosystem interface is therefore critical.

25.   The COVID-19 pandemic underlines the danger of EIDs starting from a single patient and rapidly spreading around the world in just 6 months.[22] The Centers for Disease Control and Prevention (CDC) in Atlanta lists around 50 emerging or re-emerging infectious diseases.[23] Notorious pandemics in history include the plague, smallpox, and the Spanish flu. It is estimated that the plague reduced the world population by 20% and more or less halved the European population in the 14th century. A 2002 study re-estimated the global mortality of the 1918–1920 Spanish flu at least 50 million deaths globally (2.7% of the world population).[24] A 2020 study estimates the economic losses due to the 1918–1920 Spanish flu at 7% globally.[25] Common childhood infections such as measles, diphtheria, and whooping cough annihilated nonimmune populations. With current preventive and treatment technologies, it is unlikely that such high fatality rates can happen again. However, common influenza continues to be a major cause of global annual mortality. The ongoing COVID-19 pandemic is rare and to-date the worst outbreak since the Spanish flu. However, scientists warn that pandemics of influenza and other viruses will follow, and that it is not a matter of if but when.

---

[20] The WHO defines zoonoses as diseases and infections that are naturally transmitted between vertebrate animals and humans. A zoonotic agent may be a bacterium, a virus, a fungus or other communicable disease agent.

[21] WHO. 2017. *Joint External Evaluation of IHR Core Capacities of the Islamic Republic of Pakistan*. Geneva.

[22] Communicable and infectious diseases are used interchangeably in this report.

[23] The CDC defines EID as "an infectious disease that is newly recognized as occurring in humans; one that has been recognized before but is newly appearing in a different population or geographic area than previously affected; one that is newly affecting many more individuals; and/or one that has developed new attributes (e.g., resistance or virulence)." CDC. 1995. *Emerging Infectious Diseases*. 1 (1). January–March. Georgia, United States.

[24] N. Johnson and J. Mueller. 2002. Updating the Accounts: Global Mortality of the 1918–1920 "Spanish" Influenza Pandemic. *Bulletin of the History of Medicine*. 76 (1). pp. 105–115.

[25] R. de Santis and W. van der Veken. 2020. Economic Expected Losses and Downsite Risks Due to the Spanish Flu. *Centre for Economic Policy Research*. https://voxeu.org/article/economic-expected-losses-and-downside-risks-due-spanish-flu.

26.   Following a rapid increase in the poultry population in the 1990s, avian influenza, which had been identified as the fowl plague a century earlier, infected 18 people in Hong Kong, China and the PRC in 1997, and from 2003 onwards spread globally. Sporadic cases of avian influenza continue to occur despite large control efforts.[26] The severe acute respiratory syndrome (SARS) epidemic (2002–2004), which affected CAREC countries such as Mongolia and the PRC, resulted in more than 8,000 people getting infected with a case fatality rate of about 10%.[27]

Even such a relatively small epidemic caused major economic losses. Lee and McKibbin (2004) estimated that SARS may have resulted in a loss of at least $40 billion and a gross domestic product (GDP) slowdown of 1%.[28] Later estimates are more modest but still point at a major drop in global tourism and GDP in Canada and the PRC.[29] These EIDs, like COVID-19, started in the PRC and lasted several years. Table 3 shows an overview of virus epidemics globally.

Table 3: Virus Epidemics—An Overview

Virus	Main Countries/Areas/Regions Affected	Outbreak Dates	Worldwide Cases	Deaths
SARS coronavirus	PRC; Hong Kong, China	2002 and 2003	8,096	774
Avian flu H5N1	Egypt, Indonesia	2003–2015	846	449
MERS coronavirus	Saudi Arabia, Republic of Korea	Since 2012	2,494	858
Ebola	Sierra Leone, Guinea, Liberia	2013–2016	28,616	11,310
Zika	Americas	2015 and 2020	5,822,014	...
COVID-19	Global (Pandemic)	2019 and 2021	153 million	3.2 million

... = data not available, COVID-19 = coronavirus disease, MERS = Middle East respiratory syndrome, PRC = People's Republic of China, SARS = severe acute respiratory syndrome, WHO = World Health Organization.

Sources:

SARS: WHO. Summary of Probable SARS Cases with Onset of Illness from 1 November 2002 to 31 July 2003. 2004. http://www.who.int/csr/sars/country/table2004_04_21/en/ (accessed 20 March 2020).

Avian Flu: Office International des Epizooties (OIE). Update on Avian Influenza in Animals (Type H5) 2007. http://www.oie.int/downld/AVIAN%20INFLUENZA/A_AI-Asia.htm (accessed 20 March 2020).

MERS: WHO. Middle East Respiratory Syndrome. http://www.emro.who.int/health-topics/mers-cov/mers-outbreaks.html (accessed 20 March 2020).

Ebola: WHO. Ebola Data and Statistics. https://apps.who.int/gho/data/view.ebola-sitrep.ebola-summary-latest?lang=en (accessed 20 March 2020).

Zika: WHO/Pan American Health Organization. Zika Cumulative Cases. https://www.paho.org/hq/index.php?option=com_content&view=article&id=12390:zika-cumulative-cases&Itemid=42090&lang=en (accessed 20 March 2020).

COVID-19: Johns Hopkins University. Coronavirus Resource Center. Corona Data in Motion. https://coronavirus.jhu.edu/ (accessed 3 May 2021).

---

[26]   S. Lai et al. 2016. Global Epidemiology of Avian Influenza A(H5N1) Virus Infection in Humans, 1997–2015: A Systematic Review. *The Lancet Infectious Diseases.* 16 (7). pp. e108–e118. https://www.ncbi.nlm.nih.gov/pmc/articles/PMC4933299/ Published online 2016 May 17. Doi: 10.1016/S1473-3099(16)00153-5.

[27]   WHO. Summary Table of SARS Cases by Country, 1 November 2002–7 August 2003. https://www.who.int/csr/sars/country/country2003_08_15.pdf?ua=1.

[28]   J. W. Lee and W. McKibbin. 2004. *Estimating the Global Economic Costs of SARS. Learning from SARS: Preparing for the Next Disease Outbreak: Workshop Summary.* Washington, DC.

[29]   M. R. Keogh-Brown. 2008. The Economic Impact of SARS: How does the Reality Match with the Predictions. *Health Policy.* 88 (1). October. pp. 110–120. Dublin.

27.   ADB estimates that the global economic loss inflicted by COVID-19 could reach $5.8 trillion to $8.8 trillion, or 6.4% to 9.7% of global GDP.[30] In Asia and the Pacific, COVID-19's economic impact is predicted to lead to a 0.7% contraction in aggregate economic output in 2020, the first regional GDP contraction since the 1960s.[31] The significant losses resulting from the pandemic and related containment measures involve all sectors, including aviation, tourism, trade, and other industries and sectors. As of 7 December 2020, COVID-19 has spread to 227 countries and caused more than 67 million confirmed infections and more than 1,538,000 confirmed deaths (the actual numbers are likely to be much higher due to limited testing and reporting capacity). CAREC countries (excluding Turkmenistan) reported a total of 1,309,826 confirmed cases, with 23,999 deaths by 15 December 2020 (Table 4). COVID-19 confirmed cases include not only hospitalized patients but also asymptomatic persons and those with mild symptoms.

28.   Using modeling that broadly considers the type of control measures used in each country (mitigation or suppression), projections have been made on the expected number of persons that will require hospitalization and the expected number of deaths in the pandemic, assuming no vaccine or treatment will become available soon. Based on a basic reproduction number of 3, using the best-case scenario with a 75% reduction in contacts and lockdown, in case there are more than 0.2 deaths per 100,000 population per week, a total of 2.1 million hospitalizations and 323,000 deaths

are expected in the CAREC region for the entire pandemic (Table 4).[32] By 15 December 2020, the total reported deaths reached 7.4% of the projected deaths in CAREC countries, which may have different explanations: (i) the pandemic has yet to spread and is slowed down with effective lockdown; (ii) there are limitations in surveillance, testing capacity, and reporting; (iii) the assumptions made are incorrect; or (iv) a combination of these three factors. Vaccination should substantially reduce the COVID-19 impact but there are also indications of changes in viral transmission and possibly viral pathogenicity. Compared to CAREC countries, European countries, which have good testing capacity, report much higher COVID-19 ratios. While CAREC countries differ from European countries in terms of age structure and NCD profile, an increase in COVID-19 hospitalizations must be anticipated.

29.   Responding to the threat of emerging infectious diseases requires risk reduction (prevention, preparedness, and mitigation) and resilience building at local, national, regional, and global levels. The World Health Organization (WHO) has led member countries and institutions worldwide in strengthening preparedness, surveillance, and response capacities for emerging infectious diseases and other public health issues of international concern. In 2005, World Health Organization (WHO) and member countries endorsed the revised International Health Regulations (IHR), which remain in effect with minor modifications.[33] The IHR scope is not limited to any specific disease or manner of transmission.

---

[30]   ADB. 2020. An Updated Assessment of the Economic Impact of COVID-19. *ADB Briefs No. 133*. Manila. May. https://www.adb.org/sites/default/files/publication/604206/adb-brief-133-updated-economic-impact-covid-19.pdf.

[31]   ADB. 2020. Asian Development Outlook Update. Manila. September. https://www.adb.org/sites/default/files/publication/635666/ado2020-update.pdf.

[32]   N. M. Ferguson et al. Report – 9: Impact of Non-pharmaceutical Interventions (NPIs) to Reduce COVID-19 Mortality and Healthcare Demand. Imperial College London. 16 March. https://www.imperial.ac.uk/mrc-global-infectious-disease-analysis/covid-19/report-9-impact-of-npis-on-covid-19/.

[33]   International Health Regulations are a binding instrument of international law, which 196 countries across the globe agreed to implement and which entered into force on 15 June 2007. WHO. 2005. International Health Regulations. https://www.who.int/publications/i/item/9789241580496.

Table 4: COVID-19 Cases and Deaths in Countries, as of 3 May 2021

CAREC Country	Confirmed Cases	Confirmed Deaths	Total Projected Hospitalizations[a]	Total Projected Deaths
Afghanistan	60,300	2,642	46,011	7,208
Azerbaijan	321,380	4,561	23,959	3,236
China, People's Republic of	102,532	4,846	1,445,585	219,209
Georgia	312,954	4,163	8,578	1,371
Kazakhstan	381,078	3,349	44,972	6,159
Kyrgyz Republic	96,337	1,622	14,494	1,944
Mongolia	39,381	119	6,360	933
Pakistan	834,146	18,149	434,109	73,115
Tajikistan	13,308	90	15,234	1,931
Turkmenistan	…	…	11,520	1,531
Uzbekistan	92,006	653	48,914	6,356
Total	2,253,422	40,194	2,099,736	322,993

… = data not available, CAREC = Central Asia Regional Economic Cooperation, PRC = People's Republic of China.

[a] The projections are based on a best-case scenario for non-pharmaceutical control assuming "China-like age-severity" profiles, social distancing of the whole population resulting in 75% reduction in contacts, and a suppression (lockdown) trigger at 0.2 deaths per 100,000 people per week.

Sources: Johns Hopkins University of Medicine. Coronavirus Resource Center. Corona Data in Motion. https://coronavirus.jhu.edu/ (accessed 3 May 2021).

N. M. Ferguson et al. 2020. Report 9: Impact of Non-Pharmaceutical Interventions (NPIs) To Reduce COVID-19 Mortality and Healthcare Demand. Imperial College London. 16 March. London https://www.imperial.ac.uk/mrc-global-infectious-disease-analysis/covid-19/report-9-impact-of-npis-on-covid-19/.

Governments are to develop certain minimum core public health capacities and are obliged to notify WHO of events that may constitute a public health emergency of international concern.

30.   Over the past decade, CAREC countries, led by the ministries of health, have been advancing implementation and maintenance of IHR (2005) core capacities for disease control and management. Following the IHR indicators of preparedness for emerging diseases, several countries (Afghanistan, Georgia, Kazakhstan, the Kyrgyz Republic, Mongolia, Pakistan, and Tajikistan) have conducted Joint External Evaluations (JEE) and prioritized

health crisis management and preparedness in their national plans at different levels and stages (Appendix A2.4). These efforts could be supplemented with a forecasting and modeling element, to allow for better preparedness and more accurate costing for future outbreaks and pandemics.

31.   WHO member countries conduct an annual IHR self-assessment of 13 IHR capacities using e-SPAR, a web-based self-assessment tool.[34] The WHO and its member countries also conduct JEE to validate these self-assessments.[35] As summarized in Table 5, CAREC countries report a high level of risk reduction and resilience, but at regional level,

---

[34]   WHO. e-SPAR State Party Annual Report. https://extranet.who.int/e-spar.

[35]   WHO. Joint External Evaluation (JEE) mission reports. https://www.who.int/ihr/procedures/mission-reports/en/.

Table 5: CAREC Countries, IHR Self-Assessment Score 2019

e-SPAR Indicators	AFG	AZE	PRC	GEO	KAZ	KGZ	MON	PAK	TAJ	TKM	UZB
Legislation and financing	33	80	93	67	80	53	80	27	60	60	67
IHR coordination and national IHR focal point functions	80	90	100	80	90	50	100	50	70	70	40
Zoonotic events and human–animal interface	80	80	100	80	80	80	100	60	60	100	60
Food safety	20	80	100	60	80	0	80	40	40	60	20
Laboratory	47	87	100	93	80	50	60	60	47	73	67
Surveillance	80	90	100	70	80	63	100	60	60	70	60
Human resources	40	80	100	60	80	20	80	60	60	60	60
National Health Emergency Framework	33	73	80	60	87	60	80	47	73	73	67
Health service provision	53	93	93	60	93	40	87	33	80	67	80
Risk communication	20	100	80	20	80	40	80	20	80	60	60
Points of entry	30	80	100	40	80	30	80	40	60	90	40
Chemical events	20	100	80	20	80	40	80	40	60	60	40
Radiation emergencies	20	100	80	40	80	60	80	100	60	60	80

AFG = Afghanistan, AZE = Azerbaijan, CAREC = Central Asia Regional Economic Cooperation, e-SPAR=electronic state parties' self-assessment annual reporting tool, GEO = Georgia, IHR = International Health Regulations, KAZ = Kazakhstan, KGZ = Kyrgyz Republic, MON = Mongolia, PAK = Pakistan, PRC = People's Republic of China, TAJ = Tajikistan, TKM = Turkmenistan, UZB = Uzbekistan.

Source: WHO. Strategic Partnership for International Health Regulations (2005) and Health Security (SPH). IHR States Parties Self-Assessment Annual Reporting (SPAR). https://extranet.who.int/e-spar (accessed 11 June 2020).

they score less on IHR capacities such as legislation and financing, food safety, human resources, risk communication, points of entry, and chemical events—which could be priorities for improvement.

32.   The COVID-19 pandemic is an extreme case for which no country was sufficiently prepared. Yet some important lessons can be learned. One year into the pandemic, vaccines and medicines have become available, but much remained unknown about transmission, control measures, and treatment. The impact of the COVID-19 pandemic is aggravated by a high burden of NCDs, with disastrous consequences.[36] This should encourage

countries to further strengthen their health promotion and NCD prevention programs. COVID-19 is also more difficult to control in urban slums, thereby stressing the importance of improving living conditions for the poor. In the aftermath of COVID-19, governments hope to renew their commitment toward SDGs; conduct health sector reforms; and improve sector financing for epidemic preparedness in terms of better surveillance and laboratory testing capacity, hospital surge capacity, and emergency supplies. Preventing or mitigating certain epidemics will also require improving biosafety and trade in livestock, and vaccine and medicine development capacities.

---

[36]   As stated by Carissa F Etienne, Director, Pan American Health Organization (PAHO). PAHO. 2020. Weekly Press Briefing on Covid-19, Director's Opening Remarks. 26 May. https://www.paho.org/en/documents/weekly-press-briefing-covid-19-directors-opening-remarks-may-26-2020.

Other Communicable Diseases

33   CAREC countries are also exposed to outbreaks of other communicable diseases that may spread regionally. Among the more acute infections, malaria, dengue, and Japanese encephalitis persist in Pakistan and the PRC.

34.   Chronic infectious diseases (CIDs) such as HIV/AIDS, TB, and viral hepatitis B and C also have regional impact and continue to pose a heavy burden in CAREC countries. It is important to address these diseases and their risk factors at the regional level, given their potential for crossing borders, affecting migrants, and burdening health services. HIV/AIDS is a major public health concern in the CAREC region, especially in Afghanistan, Pakistan, and the PRC. A broad range of risk factors and health determinants may have to be considered, including changing social norms, public education, migration, and unemployment.

35.   Hepatitis, in particular, viral hepatitis B and C, is highly prevalent in all CAREC countries. The PRC (14%) and Pakistan (10%) account for almost a quarter of the hepatitis C (HCV) burden among the 28 countries accounting for 80% of the HCV burden globally.[37] Mongolia also has a large incidence of chronic hepatitis B virus (HBV) and HCV infections. HCV and HBV are the predominant causes of liver cancer and cirrhosis. Liver cancer is the most common type of cancer in Mongolia and the PRC, accounting for 50% of the global burden. Vaccination for

HBV and low-cost treatment for HCV can reduce this burden.

36.   The incidence of TB, although declining across the CAREC region, continues to pose a major threat even in its uncomplicated form, especially in the form of multidrug-resistant TB (MDR-TB).[38] CAREC countries in general have a high incidence of TB. Pakistan and the PRC are on WHO's list of top 30 countries with the highest estimated numbers of TB cases (PRC) and MDR-TB cases (Pakistan); while Azerbaijan, Kazakhstan, the Kyrgyz Republic, Tajikistan, and Uzbekistan have the highest MDR-TB burden in the WHO European Region. [39,]

37.   Nosocomial (hospital acquired) infections pose an increasing public health threat with global dimensions, and are associated with poor hospital infection prevention and control, poor or inexistent quality assurance, antimicrobial resistance (AMR), and low private sector interest in developing new medicines with limited market potential. Actions are required at global, regional, and hospital levels to address these infections.

38.   AMR is the ability of microbes to resist medication, and is also associated with the inappropriate use of medicines including veterinary medicines. It is rapidly becoming a global public health challenge. [40] Drug-resistant pathogens can be transmitted between humans and animals, across health care facilities, in communities, and across country borders.

---

[37]   WHO. 2017. *Global Hepatitis Report*. Geneva.

[38]   The average TB incidence rate in the EURO WHO region declined from 5.4% in 2006–2015 to 3.3% in 2014–2015 .

[39]   According to WHO's Global TB report (2018), in 2016, the 10 countries with the highest MDR-TB ratio are (in alphabetical order) Azerbaijan, Belarus, Kazakhstan, the Kyrgyz Republic, Moldova, the Russian Federation, Somalia, Tajikistan, Ukraine, and Uzbekistan. WHO. 2018. *Global Tuberculosis Report*. Geneva.

[40]   WHO Regional Office for Europe. 2018. Better Labs for Better Health. Strengthening Laboratory Systems in the WHO European Region. Report of the 3rd Partners Meeting with a focus on Antimicrobial Resistance. Almaty, Kazakhstan. 9–10 October. https://www.euro.who.int/__data/assets/pdf_file/0003/400296/Partners-Meeting-2018-Report-en.pdf. Kazakhstan, Tajikistan, and Uzbekistan are reporting concerns about the quality of antimicrobials.

Resistance to inexpensive and effective antimicrobial drugs has emerged at an alarmingly high rate, making many common diseases and pathogens (such as TB) difficult and expensive to treat.[41] AMR requires actions at global, regional, national, and local levels including enforcement of legislation, public education, infection prevention and control, quality assurance, surveillance, and research. Detecting and responding to AMR relies on strengthened and coordinated laboratory and surveillance capacities in the region as well as coordinated responses across sectors of human and animal health, environment, trade, and intellectual property and innovation.

39.   Infectious diseases, including emerging and zoonotic infections and threats from AMR, constitute a significant regional health concern owing to their ability to rapidly spread regionally and internationally as a result of increases in connectivity and proliferation of trade. Cross-border surveillance, information sharing, and coordination across human and animal sectors are crucial to control these diseases. The transboundary nature of infections (TB, hepatitis, HIV, and animal and emerging diseases) contributes to their spread; while weak surveillance, detection, early warning, and referral systems contribute to the speed of proliferation, difficulty in preventing and controlling outbreaks, epidemics, and pandemics.

Noncommunicable Diseases

40.   As described in Section 2.1, the burden of disease in the CAREC region is dominated by NCDs. Cardiovascular diseases (CVDs)

accounted for the biggest number of NCD deaths in 2018 in CAREC, that is 4.5 million people annually; cancers accounted for 2.3 million, followed by respiratory diseases (0.9 million), and diabetes (0.2 million).[42] A large portion of these deaths have occurred in the PRC, due to its large population size (one-fifth of the global population), with 89% of deaths due to NCDs. The NCD increase is gradual for most CAREC countries, except Georgia, which has experienced a steep rise (Figure 2).

41.   NCDs and related conditions have been shown to disproportionately affect people in middle-income countries (MICs), where more than three-quarters of global NCD-related deaths occur. As measured by disability adjusted life years (DALYs) and years of life lost (YLLs), the onset of NCDs among young adults and associated costs can have devastating economic and social consequences. An analysis by the World Economic Forum estimated that the PRC loses more than 20 million productive life years to NCDs annually.[43] A 2005 study showed that tobacco use, which is an associated risk factor, increased the odds of sick leave between 32% and 56%.[44] Globally, the premature mortality associated with NCDs has declined by 1.3% per year between 1990 and 2017. On the other hand, several CAREC countries (Afghanistan, Mongolia, Pakistan, Turkmenistan, and Uzbekistan) have shown an upward trend and high levels of premature avertable mortality from NCDs.[45]

42.   The chronic nature and high treatment costs associated with most of the NCDs means patients suffer longer and require more medical

---

[41]   The human and financial costs of AMR are recognized worldwide, with estimates of 700,000 deaths each year globally due to drug-resistant infections, and projected annual reduction in GDP of 3.8% by 2050.

[42]   Institute for Health Metrics and Evaluation (IHME). 2018. *Global Burden of Disease Study Results (2017)*. Seattle, Washington. http://vizhub.healthdata.org/gbd-compare/.

[43]   World Economic Forum. 2008. *Working Towards Wellness: The Business Rationale*. Geneva.

[44]   S. Tsai et al. 2005. *Tobacco Control*. 14. pp. 33–37. https://www.ncbi.nlm.nih.gov/pmc/articles/PMC1766182/.

[45]   R. Martinez et al. 2020. Trends in Premature Avertable Mortality from Non-Communicable Diseases for 195 Countries and Territories, 1990–2017: A Population-based Study. *The Lancet*. 8 (4). April. pp. E511–E523. 1. https://doi.org/10.1016/S2214-109X(20)30035-8.

Figure 2: Noncommunicable Diseases in CAREC, 1990–2017

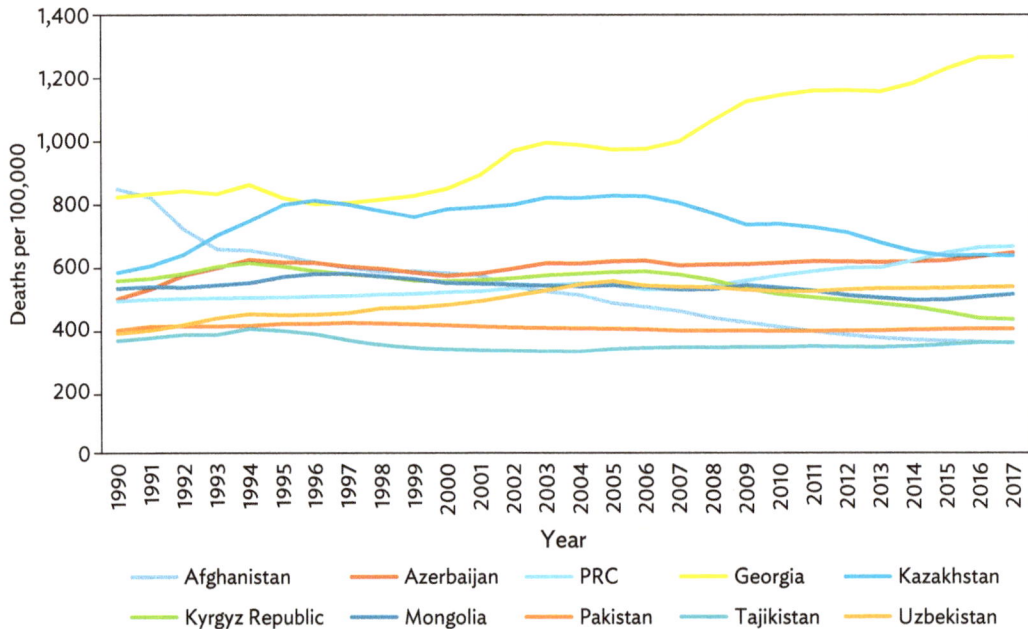

CAREC = Central Asia Regional Economic Cooperation, PRC = People's Republic of China.

Note: Data for Turkmenistan are not available.

Source: Institute for Health Metrics and Evaluation (IHME). 2018. *Global Burden of Disease Study Results (2017)*. Seattle, Washington. http://vizhub.healthdata.org/gbd-compare/.

care and hospitalization. The effects are felt at the household, national, and global level. NCDs can have a catastrophic effect on households through high out-of-pocket spending on health services and caregivers. The share of out-of-pocket spending is very high in most CAREC countries (Section 3.5) and this can quickly cause households to slip into poverty. The affected labor supply makes it harder to capitalize on the demographic dividend that would otherwise occur from having a larger proportion of young, working-age population relative to other countries. This, in turn, reduces the wealth generation and productivity that would otherwise support the countries' development and investment. At the national level, apart from economic and fiscal impact,

the high treatment costs and long treatment time undermine the ability of health care systems to tackle other health priorities. At the regional level, reduced national productivity and consumption leads to slower regional growth.

43. CAREC countries have undertaken various efforts to reduce the burden of NCDs, such as addressing child obesity in Tajikistan, promoting physical exercise in Turkmenistan, developing family medicine, and improving tertiary hospital services. However, these actions often come as projects and programs, which may undergo irregular financing and interruptions. As promoted under the SDGs and by the WHO, a multisector approach is required based on the concept of "health in all policies".[46] This is a major

---

[46] WHO Regional Office for Europe. 2018. Multisectoral and Intersectoral Actions for Improved Health and Well-Being for All: Mapping of WHO Europe Region. *Final Report*. Copenhagen.

challenge in the region because of the vertical way in which the services are organized, and will require major reforms.

44. RHC provides multiple opportunities for countries to join forces to improve sector leverage, performance, and financing. Tackling health challenges in the region will also depend on building resilient health systems. Key health systems issues and development in the region are discussed in Section 2.4.

Migration

45. Increasing labor migration coupled with challenges from infectious and emerging diseases in the region further contribute to an

increased threat of outbreaks and pandemics.[47] In 2019, about 10.3 million migrants from CAREC countries worked outside their home countries (Table 6). Cultural and structural barriers and lack of insurance coverage often deter migrants from obtaining necessary and timely care, resulting in increased health care burdens from higher treatment costs (in comparison to prevention and early detection).[48] Labor migrants, particularly the unskilled and undocumented, are often in poor working and living conditions. They work under limited social protection and have poor access to health and other social services.[49] These circumstances in turn may contribute to health hazards, especially infectious diseases. As evidenced in Tajikistan and Uzbekistan, foreign workers are more

Table 6: International Migrant Stock in CAREC Countries, 2019

Indicators	AFG	AZE	PRC	GEO	KAZ	KGZ	MON	PAK	TAJ	TKM	UZB
Number of migrants[a] (in thousands)	149.8	253.9	1,030.9	79.0	3,705.6	200.3	21.1	3,258.0	274.1	195.1	1,168.4
Migrants as % of national population	0.4	2.5	0.1	2.0	20.0	3.1	0.7	1.5	2.9	3.3	3.5
Female migrants as % of all migrants	49.9	52.1	38.6	56.2	50.4	59.6	33.2	47.4	56.9	52.7	53.4
Type of data[b]	B	B, R	C	B	B	B	C	B, R	B	B	B

AFG = Afghanistan, AZE = Azerbaijan, CAREC = Central Asia Regional Economic Cooperation, GEO = Georgia, KAZ = Kazakhstan, KGZ = Kyrgyz Republic, MON = Mongolia, PAK = Pakistan, PRC = People's Republic of China, TAJ = Tajikistan, TKM = Turkmenistan, UZB = Uzbekistan.

[a] Totals are only an estimate as the number of informal migrants cannot be accurately counted.

[b] This row indicates the data used to produce the estimates: (B) foreign-born population, (C) foreign citizens, and (R) refugees.

Source: United Nations Department of Economic and Social Affairs. International Migration. https://www.un.org/en/development/desa/population/migration/data/estimates2/estimates19.asp (accessed 16 January 2020).

[47] B. Babamuradov et al. 2017. Reducing TB Among Central Asia Migrants. *Health Affairs*. 36 (9). 1688. 1 September. https://www.healthaffairs.org/doi/full/10.1377/hlthaff.2017.0794.

[48] *International Federation for Human Rights*. 2017. Migrant Workers in Central Asia are Subjected to High Migration Costs. 8 June. https://www.fidh.org/en/region/europe-central-asia/migrant-workers-in-central-asia-are-subjected-to-high-migration-costs.

[49] N. El-Bassel et al. 2011. Implications of Mobility Patterns and HIV Risks for HIV Prevention Among Migrant Market Vendors in Kazakhstan. *American Journal of Public Health*. 101 (6). pp. 1075–1081. June. https://www.ncbi.nlm.nih.gov/pmc/articles/PMC3093276/. Colombia University.

vulnerable to contracting HIV/AIDS.[50] Poorly ventilated and cramped living conditions and lack of access to diagnostic and treatment services contribute to a heightened risk of TB infection among labor migrants, and cross-border outbreaks. The incidence of TB and multidrug- and extensively drug-resistant TB is 2.5 times higher among labor migrants than among the general population, according to the Central Tuberculosis Research Institute of the Russian Academy of Medical Science (footnote 47). This is further exacerbated by MDR strains that are much harder and much more expensive to treat, and lack of access to information and prevention services can further exacerbate these risks.[51]

46.   While migration offers benefits, such as job opportunities and economic prosperity, it is important that related health challenges are managed collaboratively.[52] Since remittances from migrant workers constitute an important income source in the region (particularly in the Kyrgyz Republic, Pakistan, and Tajikistan), provision of health care to migrants can bring significant benefits not only to the migrants themselves, but also to their host countries and countries of origin. Evidence in the European Union shows that "timely treatment in a primary health care setting (for migrants) entails potential cost savings of at least 49% to 100% of direct medical and nonmedical costs, and between 4% to 100% of indirect costs incurred in a hospital setting for treatment of more severe medical conditions."[53] Reducing structural barriers to migrants' access to health care can positively impact the host countries' public health and, in the long run, minimize their financial burden.

2.4 Health Systems Development in the Region

47.   This section reviews the strengths and weaknesses of the health systems in CAREC countries using the six WHO-designated building blocks (Figure 4). Appendix 2 contains the full review of the strengths and weaknesses of the health systems in CAREC countries. The health systems building blocks represent the state of the national health care systems. They are all interconnected and indicate the performance levels in terms of quality, efficiency, equity, and sustainability.

48.   Health service delivery systems are diverse across the CAREC region. While there are differences in investment in health facilities, all countries essentially have health systems in transition. Many countries in the region are moving from public provider to public-private mix, from a centralized to a decentralized system, and from a focus on hospital services to investing more in primary health care. Most of the former Soviet Union republics, following independence, have gone through a rationalization process

---

[50]   Y. Amirkhanian et al. 2015. Male Labor Migrants in [the Russian Federation]: HIV Risk Behavior Levels, Contextual Factors, and Prevention Needs. *Journal of Immigration Minority Health*. 13 (5). p. 919–928.

[51]   Knowledge of HIV is lower among migrants in Central Asia than in the receiving countries (e.g., Kazakhstan, the Russian Federation). Statistical Agency under the President of the Republic of Tajikistan. 2017. Tajikistan Demographic and Health Survey (TjDHS). Dushanbe. https://microdata.worldbank.org/index.php/catalog/3394.

[52]   B. Gushulak and D. MacPherson. 2004. Globalization of Infectious Diseases: The Impact of Migration. *Clinical Infectious Diseases*. 15 June. 38 (12). pp. 1742–1748.

[53]   U. Trummer et al. 2015. *Cost Analysis of Health Care Provision for Migrants and Ethnic Minorities*. Vienna.

Figure 3: World Health Organization's Building Blocks of Health Systems

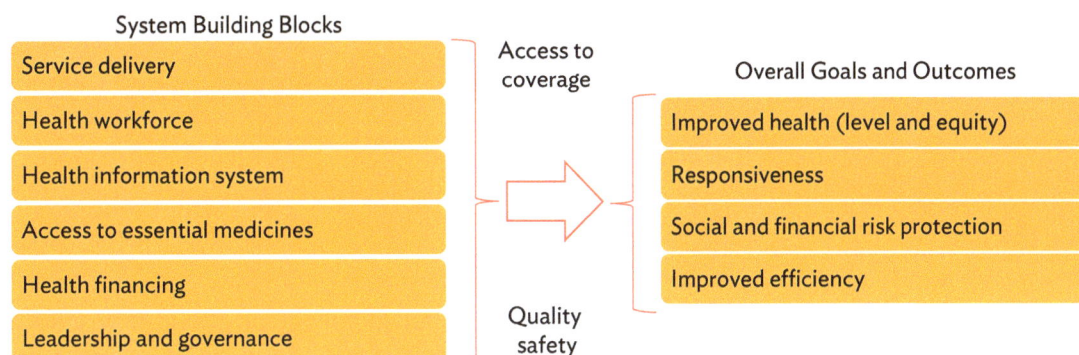

System Building Blocks

- Service delivery
- Health workforce
- Health information system
- Access to essential medicines
- Health financing
- Leadership and governance

Access to coverage

Quality safety

Overall Goals and Outcomes

- Improved health (level and equity)
- Responsiveness
- Social and financial risk protection
- Improved efficiency

Source: WHO. 2010. *Monitoring the Building Blocks of Health Systems: A Handbook of Indicators and their Measurement Strategies.* https://www.who.int/healthinfo/systems/monitoring/en/.

in terms of hospital and health staff, and have strongly promoted family medicine. These countries have typically retained a two-pillar system of clinical and sanitary services. Most CAREC countries have greater access to health services although in rural areas large sections of the population still lacks access to essential health services. Where health care is accessible, it is often fragmented and of poor quality due to workforce and other resource constraints. Absence of high quality laboratory services remains a challenge across the region.

49.   Quality improvement of health services could be a major challenge in the region in years to come. Focus should be given on developing quality improvement systems, producing high-quality workforce, and quality control of medicines—which would all require system development and regulation. Cooperation can help align laboratory and facility standards with the best international practices to standardize services.

50.   CAREC countries have implemented different strategies to optimize their human resources for health (HRH), especially through investment in producing family medicine and

primary health care doctors and nurses. Despite significant efforts, CAREC countries still face HRH challenges such as an aging workforce, inappropriate staff mix and recruitment policies, urban–rural maldistribution and retention issues, substandard quality of education, weak enforcement of standards and accreditation, poor absorption capacity, poor career structure, and substandard working environment. Facilitating the flow of health workers in the region such as through mutual recognition of skills and information sharing can help build resilience of the health workforce, and mitigate the risk of "brain drain" in the region. While a regional labor market is desirable, the region is experiencing an outflow of trained health care professionals, exacerbating the existing imbalances.

51.   Knowledge sharing helps motivate and improve competencies of public health professionals. Existing regional training programs such as sharing clinical expertise knowledge (e.g., between Pakistan and the PRC) and eLearning programs can be expanded to benefit regional health care workers with improved access to data collection and analysis and enhanced diagnostic and clinical decision-making.

52.   National health information systems in the CAREC region are typically fragmented due to parallel disease surveillance systems, lack of integration of the private sector, and fragmentation between facilities at national, provincial, and local level. This fragmentation makes data collection, analysis, and reporting challenging and impedes evidenced-based decision-making. Oftentimes, data are not sex-disaggregated, making it difficult to retrieve information on women's health status. Many countries have undertaken efforts to integrate the different systems, and introduce software to improve data collection and analysis. Regional centers of medical statistics and information have been set up and equipped to further improve the outcomes. However, interoperable health information systems require significant investment, and implementation has been limited due to inadequate material and financial resources and insufficient coordination between disparate investments. Streamlining and coordination of infectious disease surveillance at the national level will be needed to enable cooperation and information exchange at the regional level.

53.   Several trends on quality, availability, and affordability of medicines require regional attention. A major concern is the trade in substandard and fake medicines, and related over-the-counter sale and incorrect use that contribute to the emergence of drug resistance. There is a clear need to build and strengthen regulatory and quality assurance systems and capacities across the region, and reinforce the regulatory environment to provide regional quality control. Another concern is the high cost of branded pharmaceuticals. Joint investments could also increase domestic pharmaceutical production, while jointly procuring medicines could secure lower prices.

54.   The CAREC region faces several challenges in health finance including (i) a large and increasing burden of NCDs, (ii) increased funding required to achieve universal health coverage and the SDGs, and (iii) underdeveloped insurance systems. In terms of mitigating the financial burden of health services on their citizens, CAREC countries are at different stages of increasing public and private health insurance and coverage, and providing health care with government guaranteed basic packages. With the dwindling donor support and increased financial burden, less endowed CAREC countries have to find other effective ways to shoulder the financial burden, including larger national and regional private sector participation.

55.   In terms of leadership and governance, countries from the former Soviet Union have demonstrated a strong commitment to the health sector. A variety of health sector models are emerging, ranging from a predominantly public health system to a health system based on private practitioners. These health systems are still in transition, such as in terms of public–private mix, health insurance, hospital autonomy, and human resources development. CAREC countries are also strengthening their monitoring information systems to better track their progress toward achieving health results.

3

OPPORTUNITIES FOR REGIONAL HEALTH COOPERATION

56. Based on the analysis of health sector trends and health systems development in the CAREC region, the following chapter discusses opportunities for RHC. The chapter will examine drivers and constraints of RHC, provide lessons learned along types of regional cooperation and discuss opportunities and examples for three identified areas: (i) strengthening regional health security (RHS); (ii) supporting health systems development through regional cooperation; and (iii) improving health care for migrants, mobile populations, and border communities. A SWOT analysis of health sector development and cooperation in the CAREC region is available in Appendix 3. An overview of RHC examples from across the globe is provided in Appendix 4.

3.1 Drivers and Constraints of Regional Health Cooperation

57. Regional and cross-border cooperation is driven by joint regional interests and benefits (direct and indirect). Successful regional cooperation depends on factors such as leadership, consensus among parties, technical capacity, and resources (time and money). Economic rationales for regional cooperation include (i) generating commitment, competition, and leverage; (ii) economies of scale to improve services and efficiency; (iii) knowledge and technology transfer for analysis, policy making, and capacity building; and (iv) provision of regional public goods and services with externalities that are particularly important in the health sector.[54]

58. Cooperation is a general terminology referring to various parties working together, and may involve (i) communication, aimed at sharing information; (ii) coordination, wherein each party aims to improve its efficiency; (iii) cooperation, where parties share a common goal or benefit; and (iv) collaboration, for parties to create more together.[55] The more intense the cooperation is, the more complex it is likely to be. National government officers are commonly overloaded with work and preoccupied with national priorities and risks. Hence, the feasibility of regional cooperation must be assessed, plans carefully formulated, and resources assured to move beyond workshops and achieve tangible results.

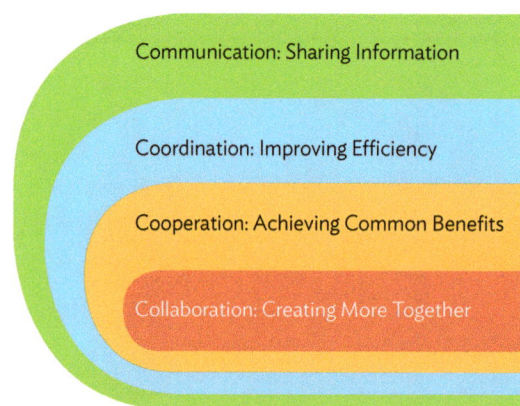

Figure 4: Four Types of Cooperation

Communication: Sharing Information

Coordination: Improving Efficiency

Cooperation: Achieving Common Benefits

Collaboration: Creating More Together

Source: Author's adaptation from a presentation by J. Hopkins. 2008. Regional Workshop on Cross-Border Collaboration in Communicable Diseases Surveillance and Response among Cambodia, People's Republic of China, Lao People's Democratic Republic and Viet Nam. 8-10 April. Da Nang.

---

[54] ADB. 2015. *Support for Regional Cooperation and Integration: Thematic Evaluation Study*. Manila.

[55] Author's adaptation from a presentation by J. Hopkins. 2008. Regional Workshop on Cross-Border Collaboration in Communicable Diseases Surveillance and Response among Cambodia, People's Republic of China, Lao People's Democratic Republic and Viet Nam. 8-10 April. Da Nang.

59.   This section describes the driving factors behind the processes that trigger, facilitate, or hinder RHC, with relevance to the CAREC region. Careful analysis, consensus building, and planning will help ensure that RHC provides added value to participating countries. Regional cooperation has four dimensions: (i) cultural and social, (ii) geographic and demographic, (iii) regulatory, and (iv) economic and technological. Each dimension includes one or more potential driving factors for cross-border health care collaboration. The dimensions and key drivers for RHC are analyzed here and summarized in Table 7.

60.   **Cultural and social dimension.** This includes mostly "external" factors such as language, habits, practices, or history. Health cooperation is more likely to happen between countries with similar welfare and health system, and close historical and cultural ties.[56] These ties generate at least mutual interest, if not bonding, stimulus, and a sense of healthy competition among countries. It is also easier for countries with similar health system rules and guidelines (e.g., vaccination schedules, etc.) to collaborate and patients would be more comfortable with familiar systems when they cross borders to receive care. Most CAREC countries share the Semashko legacy and a lingua franca (Russian). During the Soviet Union era, many Central Asian republics bought vaccines and immunization supplies from the Russian Federation; and this arrangement continued despite subsequent political changes.

61.   **Geographic dimension.** This covers the location of a country or region and its characteristics (e.g., country size, terrain, number and kinds of borders). RHC is more likely to take place in countries that are geographically connected, which makes cross-border services (e.g., health services) more accessible. Geographically isolated regions are more inclined to engage in cross-border collaboration. New technologies (e.g., telemedicine) have a bigger role to serve this group. Examples in the CAREC region include cross-border provision of telemedicine services between Afghanistan, the Kyrgyz Republic, Pakistan, and Tajikistan, as well as the international hospital in Urumqi (PRC) that has established a cross-border telemedicine platform with five neighboring countries.[57] Similar demographic factors such as population (e.g., aging population and migrants) can drive RHC through joint research and collective approaches in responding to issues with common characteristics. In CAREC, Kazakhstan (and the Russian Federation) attracts migrant labor from neighboring Central Asian countries due to different population compositions while the PRC attracts migrant labor due to its rapidly aging population.

62.   **Regulatory dimension.** This covers legal issues for cross-border collaboration, including formal and informal agreements, and legal compatibilities between parties. CAREC countries have signed a number of agreements on health cooperation: (i) international agreements such as the IHR or the WHO Framework Convention on Tobacco Control (FCTC) that build a common global health policy framework, (ii) regional agreements such as the Eurasian Economic Union (EAEU) common pharmaceutical market agreement, and (iii) bilateral agreements such as between Kazakhstan and the Kyrgyz Republic. An overview of existing agreements and regional cooperation in health can be found in Appendix 5.

---

[56]   J. Bobek et al. 2018. *Study on Cross-Border Cooperation. Capitalising on Existing Initiatives for Cooperation in Cross-border Regions.* Luxembourg: Publications Office of the European Union. https://ec.europa.eu/health/sites/health/files/cross_border_care/docs/2018_crossbordercooperation_frep_en.pdf; and I.A. Glinos and M. Wismar 2013. *Hospitals and Borders: Seven Case Studies on Cross-Border Collaboration and Health System Interactions.* Brussels: European Observatory on Health Systems and Policies.

[57]   *Belt and Road News.* 2019. Xinjiang's Int'l Hospital to Provide Cross-Border Health Services. 20 August. https://www.beltandroad.news/2019/08/20/xinjiangs-intl-hospital-to-provide-cross-border-health-services/.

Table 7: Drivers and Constraints of Regional Health Cooperation in CAREC

Driving Factors	CAREC Context
Cultural and Social Dimension	
• Cultural proximity (languages, cultural and historical heritage) • Health-related cultural proximity (type of welfare system, similarity of schedules and approaches) • Characteristics of health care services (e.g., share of out-of-pocket spending, public–private sector mix) • Health care personnel and general population mobility	• Common "Semashko" legacy (8 of 11 countries). Despite these countries undertaking very different reform paths, this common legacy still offers a potential springboard for strengthening regional collaboration in CAREC. • Commonly spoken language of importance (Russian) • Creation of mutual interest and healthy competition • High out-of-pocket spending across the region with a few exceptions • Health care personnel crossing borders in search of better education and economic opportunities
Geographic and Demographic Dimension	
• Population composition (aging population, migration) • Population characteristics (e.g., epidemiology) • Borders and border areas across CAREC countries • Regional and country isolation, ruggedness of terrain, difficulty in accessing the region or country	• Multiple borders of significant length • Many "porous" borders crossed unofficially by regional traders and livestock • Mountain terrains and isolated CAREC border regions (e.g., Afghanistan, Tajikistan, the Kyrgyz Republic) • CAREC countries at different stages of demographic transition (significant aging population and significant young population in different countries) • Large migration flows due to economic and demographic imbalances • Epidemiological similarity based on the growing NCD burden (and associated risk factors) and the infectious diseases burden (HIV, hepatitis, EIDs)
Regulatory Dimension	
• Legal and regulatory provisions (national, bilateral, regional, and global agreements on cooperation) • Data protection provisions	• Multiple regional and bilateral agreements (e.g., among WHO European Region countries, CIS countries, EAEU countries, and countries under bilateral economic corridors (China–Pakistan Economic Corridor [CPEC] and Almaty–Bishkek Economic Corridor [ABEC])
Economic and Technological Dimension	
• Market failure for regional public goods requires government intervention and regional collaboration • Socioeconomic linkages • Economies of scale (increased specialization, pooling of competencies and resources, cost reduction, and quality of care) • Technology uptake in countries and region • Innovative capacity • Use of ICT (mobile and eHealth, digital literacy)	• Control of emerging and other diseases spreading across borders requires regional collaboration • Creation of employment opportunities and cost reduction from provision of cross-border care and services (e.g., cross-border infrastructure such as hospitals) • Efficiency gains and positive externalities from information sharing and cooperation in education and training of human resources for health • Economies of scale through aggregated demand, joint procurement of medicines and technologies • Uptake of mobile and eHealth at the regional level (telemedicine projects: Pakistan–PRC, Afghanistan–Kyrgyz Republic–Pakistan–Tajikistan) • Use and adoption of innovative technologies and ICT

CAREC = Central Asia Regional Economic Cooperation, CIS = Commonwealth of Independent States, EAEU = Eurasian Economic Union, EID = emerging infectious disease, ICT = information and communication technology, NCD = noncommunicable disease, PRC = People's Republic of China, WHO = World Health Organization.

Source: Author adapted from J. Bobek et al. 2018. *Study on Cross-Border Cooperation. Capitalizing on Existing Initiatives for Cooperation in Cross-Border Regions.* https://ec.europa.eu/health/sites/health/files/cross_border_care/docs/2018_crossbordercooperation_frep_en.pdf.

63. **Economic and technological dimension.** This covers social and economic aspects, economies of scale effects (economic dimension), and technological capacity to innovate and the use of ICT (technological dimension). An important rationale for regional collaboration in health is that infectious diseases cross borders, thus their control is a public good that requires government intervention and cooperation among countries. Arguments on economic dimension for regional cooperation include positive and negative externalities. An example of positive externality is knowledge sharing in addressing EIDs, which can lead to better prevention and control policies, and lower human and financial burden. Negative externality, on the other hand, may include smuggling and inconsistent tobacco taxation among countries with common borders, which increases tobacco consumption despite the introduction of more stringent national tobacco tax policies.

64. Economies of scale can be achieved through regional cooperation, such as joint research to address rare diseases, and joint procurement, also known as group purchasing, which is especially relevant for small countries without the purchasing power of larger nations. In CAREC, a few countries (e.g., Kazakhstan, Pakistan, and the PRC) whose domestic pharmaceutical industry is rapidly developing may be well-positioned to supply drugs efficiently through regional agreements. Collective bargaining for group purchase can be undertaken if the production (or prevention of production and use) of a good (e.g., drugs, food labeling, tobacco labeling) is more efficient when all countries participate. In the case of food labeling and regulating contents of processed foods, it may be less costly to have a uniform industrial approach in the entire region than to label and process them differently in each country.

65. RHC can take many forms. In the context of trade, regional cooperation can mean coordination of policies and measures that improve the flow of goods (e.g., medicines, medical equipment, and supplies), people (e.g., health professionals, nurses, physicians, and students), services (e.g., telehealth and telemedicine), and knowledge (e.g., knowledge transfer to improve pharmaceutical production practice and domestic manufacturing capacities). The movement of skilled health personnel and knowledge across borders would improve CAREC health labor markets, and benefit the region and individual countries.

66. The substantial costs addressing EIDs and TADs make it urgent for countries to introduce and strengthen measures at national and regional levels, particularly in responding to pandemics like COVID-19. Many CAREC countries have already invested in improving the prevention and treatment of EIDs and TADs through enhanced infrastructure and PHC services, improved surveillance, and overall compliance to International Health Regulations (IHR) (2005). Disease prevention and control calls for national mitigation measures and regional cooperation and integration (RCI) initiatives. Several CAREC countries (e.g., Kazakhstan, the Kyrgyz Republic, and Tajikistan) have introduced bilateral agreements related to cross-border TB prevention and control to facilitate surveillance and referral of infectious diseases.[58] Global and regional initiatives have been undertaken to strengthen health security through the Global Health Security Agenda (GHSA) and to enhance human–animal health collaboration through One Health initiative. Experiences have demonstrated that cross-country initiatives can encourage and sustain national efforts.

---

[58] *Stop TB Partnership.* 2017. Central Asia Addresses Cross–Border Tuberculosis Prevention and Control Among Migrants. 10 April. http://www.stoptb.org/news/frompartners/2017/fp17_015.asp.

3.2 Types of Regional Cooperation and Lessons Learned

67.   Based on the drivers and SWOT analysis, various types of regional cooperation in health can be considered. The economic rationale, important feasibility issues, and lessons learned have yielded some insights to consider when enhancing CAREC's regional cooperation in health. They are highlighted below.

68.   **Generating commitment, competition, and leverage.** Based on historical and socioeconomic linkages, common legacy, and existing regional cooperation, there is a strong common interest to work together to advance the region and use the leverage of a region to negotiate with the global community, especially in achieving UHC and the SDGs, and in controlling EIDs. A healthy professional competition exists among most of the CAREC countries to do better and show improvements in the health sector. In the Greater Mekong Subregion (GMS) communicable diseases control program, the participation of health professionals in regional events has been an important stimulus for improving national performance. Holding annual workshops has helped inform and motivate leaders. Regional cooperation has attracted substantial funding beyond what countries could mobilize individually.

69.   **Economies of scale to improve services and efficiency.** Economies of scale is a straightforward rationale for regional cooperation, but experience shows that this is not easy to achieve, partly because decision-making is often not based on economies of scale but on administrative requirements. Joint health services are a logical approach to improve capacity and quality for specialist services, cross-border services, and migrant health services including insurance. The CAREC region already has some examples of joint specialized services.

For migrant health services, experiences are mixed. Special arrangements need to be carefully designed to improve migrants' access to local health services.

70.   **Knowledge and technology transfer for capacity building.** Knowledge and technology transfer that continues on a daily basis, whether intentional or not, is a great driver of regional cooperation. It could be in the form of routine sharing of scientific information, scholarships, mentoring, study tours, research, and policy advice. It is less sensitive than specific service information sharing but depends on the willingness of entities to share their knowledge, and common interests such as generating goodwill, improving business, and preventing the spread of infectious diseases across borders. Knowledge and technology transfer is particularly important in addressing the wide knowledge and capacity gaps in the health sector. Considerable knowledge and best practices exist within the region that can be harnessed and exchanged between countries.

71.   **Regional public goods and services with externalities.** The control of communicable diseases is an obvious priority choice for regional cooperation as these diseases cross borders and require joint efforts to bring them under control. The twin realities are, however, that regional disease control requires the contribution of all countries to be effective and efficient, and that a substantial part of regional disease control is the improvement of national health systems. More intense cooperation such as for cross-border disease control, or collaboration in joint studies must deal with administrative and financial constraints.

72.   **Summary of lessons learned.** The key lessons learned here are the need to (i) develop

regional and cross-border cooperation step by step; (ii) ensure viable plans with assessments, buy-in from stakeholders, clear agreements, pilots, and sustainable funding; examine financing mechanisms; and propose realistic programming; (iii) seek institutional partnerships such as between national communicable diseases control institutions or with third parties and where feasible, build on existing initiatives;

(iv) facilitate with regional oversight, focal points, and a secretariat; (v) institutionalize and further strengthen RHC at national level as an essential part of the health sector structure, staff responsibilities, and budget; and (vi) assess the value addition of regional health initiatives vis-à-vis national-level solutions. These elements have, for example, helped shape the GMS regional health program.

3.3 Priorities for Regional Cooperation

73.   Based on the previous analysis, this section discusses priorities and opportunities for RHC for three overall and interlinked objectives that can serve as entry points for RHC: (i) strengthening RHS; (ii) supporting health systems development through regional cooperation; and (iii) improving health care for migrants, mobile populations, and border communities. For each of these regional objectives, several opportunities are put forward, taking into account ownership, rationale, potential impact, and feasibility based on lessons learned in CAREC and elsewhere. This is not an exhaustive list of priorities, and other areas for regional cooperation could be added.

Strengthening Regional Health Security

74.   EIDs and TADs, and other communicable diseases, given their transboundary nature and sometimes fast spread and case fatality, pose a significant burden and threat to human activities and economic growth in the CAREC region. The COVID-19 experience reconfirms the importance of investing in RHS as a regional public good to mitigate large scale health and socioeconomic impact. Even

before the outbreak of COVID-19, CAREC countries have been undertaking multiple efforts in improving RHS through national, regional, and global actions. Such efforts need to be sustained and strengthened to improve pandemic preparedness, and control the spread of emerging and chronic infectious diseases in the region.

75.   As described in Chapter 2, the WHO developed the national self-assessment and JEE tools to assess country-level capacity to prevent, detect, and rapidly respond to health security threats to inform countries' investments in global health security interventions. JEE requires voluntary country participation, transparency, and openness of data and information sharing. While metrics like JEE measure the national capacities, the IHR (2005) also encourage countries to strengthen regional collaboration. For example, instead of requiring that countries establish reference laboratories capable of undertaking all the diagnostic tests for national priority diseases, it is enough to have an established agreement and relationship with a regional or international reference laboratory for the diagnosis.[59]

---

59   WHO. 2018. *Joint External Evaluation Tool—International Health Regulations (2005), Second Edition.* https://www.who.int/ihr/publications/WHO_HSE_GCR_2018_2/en/.

76.   Currently, CAREC countries lack a comprehensive strategy to help implement IHR, but WHO Europe provides guidelines for each subsector. IHR (2005) has had minor amendments to broaden the scope but requires further revisions, especially to speed up response time in view of global connectivity. The WHO and other United Nations agencies also provide an array of guidelines, standards, and tools for RHS which, as reflected in e-SPAR, require localization. For example, the WHO South-East Asia Regional Office and Western Pacific Regional Office are currently implementing the third phase of the Asia Pacific Strategy for Emerging Diseases (APSED III).[60]

77.   Based on the IHR (2005) legislation, endorsed by all WHO member countries, 13 technical areas have been identified. Priorities and opportunities for RHS in CAREC are discussed along the 13 technical areas.

Legislation and Financing

78.   The WHO IHR provides the global policy framework for emergency preparedness and response, which has been adopted by all CAREC WHO member states. IHR legislation particularly focuses on EIDs and classic epidemic diseases like cholera, meningitis, plague, yellow fever, certain childhood infections, TADs, and AMR. Other infectious diseases that may spread regionally like HIV/AIDS, tuberculosis, malaria, dengue, and neglected tropical diseases may be considered if these have reached epidemic proportions based on IHR criteria.[61]

79.   Linked with global, regional, and bilateral initiatives, CAREC countries have various RHS related collaborations in place. A selection is shown in Box 1.

80.   The International Federation of the Red Cross and Red Crescent Societies (IFRC) has been assisting GMS countries in reviewing and recommending the country legal framework for emergencies. The experience is that during emergencies, there are all kinds of legal issues that are better resolved in advance, so as not to waste time during emergencies. CAREC countries have been advancing legal preparedness with the help of WHO, but more needs to be done.

81.   IHR are not being fully implemented due to insufficient institutionalization in the public health sector. Institutionalization of IHR would require administrative structure, modest but regular annual operational budget, and staff resources; hence the e-SPAR criteria were revised to emphasize sustainable financing. Without administrative arrangements, sustainable funds, and staff resources, the entire IHR implementation is at risk. The challenge of these three areas is mostly not in planning but in implementation.

82.   On financing, all CAREC countries have been investing in their respective national health systems. Some countries have regional investments to support cross-border health services (e.g., cross-border telemedicine) such as through regional agreements. The COVID-19 pandemic has sharply accelerated this national development. Based on WHO epidemic preparedness assessment and planning guidelines, (i) various scenarios were projected; (ii) shortcomings in surveillance, testing, and treatment capacities were identified; and (iii) plans and budgets were prepared in coordination with partners to mobilize emergency support for the health sector and mitigate social, economic, and fiscal impact.

---

[60]   WHO SEARO and WPRO. 2017. *Asia Pacific Strategy for Emerging Diseases and Public Health Emergencies (APSED III): Advancing Implementation of the International Health Regulations (2005): Working Together Towards Health Security.* Geneva.

[61]   IHR. Frequently Asked Questions. https://www.who.int/ihr/about/FAQ2009.pdf?ua=1.

Box 1: International Health Regulations (2005) Related Initiatives in CAREC Countries

Sendai Framework for Disaster Risk Reduction 2015–2030 of the United Nations Office for Disaster Risk Reduction. The Sendai Framework outlines seven clear targets and four priorities for action to prevent new and reduce existing disaster risks: (i) understanding disaster risk; (ii) strengthening disaster risk governance to manage disaster risk; (iii) investing in disaster reduction for resilience; and (iv) enhancing disaster preparedness for effective response, and to "Build Back Better" in recovery, rehabilitation, and reconstruction. It aims to achieve the substantial reduction of disaster risk and losses in lives, livelihoods and health, and in the economic, physical, social, cultural and environmental assets of persons, businesses, communities, and countries over the next 15 years.[a]

Global Health Security Agenda. The Global Health Security Agenda (GHSA) is a global network of 69 countries, international and nongovernment organizations, and private sector companies to accelerate progress toward a world safe and secure from infectious disease threats; to promote global health security as an international priority; and to spur progress toward full implementation of the IHR, the performance of Veterinary Services Pathways, and other relevant global health security frameworks. Among the CAREC countries, current GHSA members are Afghanistan, Azerbaijan, Georgia, Mongolia, Pakistan, and the People's Republic of China (PRC), while Kazakhstan, the Kyrgyz Republic, Tajikistan, and Uzbekistan have also received support from the GHSA.[b]

The Health Silk Road under the Belt and Road Initiative. This is an initiative led by the PRC and introduced in 2017 to strengthen and renew ancient links between cultures and people, with health at its core.[c]

One Health. Afghanistan, Azerbaijan, Georgia, Kazakhstan, and Pakistan have endorsed and implemented the One Health approach, a global approach for collaboration of sectors for infectious diseases control introduced by the World Organisation for Animal Health and the World Health Organization. It is based on understanding risks for human and animal health (including both domestic animals and wildlife) and ecosystems as a whole.[d]

CAREC Common Agenda for Modernization of Sanitary and Phytosanitary measures for Trade.
This is a regional CAREC initiative that promotes regional trade in agriculture through alignment of sanitary and phytosanitary measures with international standards.[e]

CAREC = Central Asia Regional Economic Cooperation.

[a] United Nations Office for Risk Reduction. *Sendai Framework for Disaster Risk Reduction 2015-2030*. https://www.undrr.org/publication/sendai-framework-disaster-risk-reduction-2015-2030.

[b] Global Health Security Agenda. https://ghsagenda.org/.

[c] K. Tang et al. 2017. China's Silk Road and Global Health. *The Lancet*. December. 390 (10112). pp. 2595–2601.

[d] World Organisation for Animal Health. One Health "At a Glance". https://www.oie.int/en/for-the-media/onehealth/.

[e] CAREC. 2015. CAREC Common Agenda for Modernization of Sanitary and Phytosanitary Measures for Trade. https://www.carecprogram.org/uploads/CAREC-Common-Agenda-Modernization-SPS-Measures-Trade.pdf.

Source: Author's summary.

---

83.   In 2020, several CAREC country projects and programs were approved for financing the COVID-19 response, which has dramatically changed the financing of RHS. These projects are also designed to strengthen resilience to future regional health threats by improving surveillance, laboratories, and hospital intensive care capacity. There are considerable technical, socioeconomic, and financial risks with such a rapid investment, including operations and maintenance that need to be planned for the health sector in the aftermath of COVID-19. There is a need to strategically leverage these investments generated through COVID-19 response to strengthen health security capabilities and build resilient health systems.

IHR Coordination and Regional Cooperation

84.   The next priority area is IHR coordination and country focal point. The WHO is responsible for overall IHR coordination but has been impeded to fully roll out regional support due to resource constraints. Country focal points have been established, including at regional and district levels. Integration of IHR and other disease control may require improvement. Currently, there is no overall coordination mechanism across all CAREC countries like a working group for health, and a regional knowledge hub. At the same time, CAREC countries have several tripartite and bilateral agreements in place and several international, regional and local organizations are engaged in subregional and cross-border initiatives in health security that CAREC can build on and learn from. One of them is the Shanghai Cooperation Organization (Box 2).

85.   Several issues need to be considered for IHR coordination and regional cooperation:

(i)   Strong country ownership is needed for regional networks.[62]

(ii)   Collaboration with agencies such as the WHO and other global initiatives that are already supporting IHR coordination are needed.

(iii)   RHS performance depends on the weakest part of any national health system contributing to RHS, or conversely, strong national health systems constitute a major share in RHS. For example, investing in improving national data collection, laboratory capacity, training of health professionals, and regulation of health facilities provides some of the necessary conditions for regional health surveillance. A responsive national health system has a positive spillover effect that reduces the incidence of infectious diseases nationally,

---

Box 2: The Shanghai Cooperation Organization

The Shanghai Cooperation Organization (SCO) is an intergovernmental organization established on 15 June 2011 to safeguard security and stability across the vast Eurasian region, join forces to counteract emerging challenges and threats, and enhance trade and cultural and humanitarian cooperation. The SCO's original members include Kazakhstan, the Kyrgyz Republic, the People's Republic of China, the Russian Federation, Tajikistan, and Uzbekistan. India and Pakistan became members in 2017. Afghanistan, Belarus, Iran, and Mongolia are observer states. The dialogue partners are Azerbaijan, Armenia, Cambodia, Nepal, Turkey, and Sri Lanka. The secretariat is based in Beijing, PRC. The coronavirus disease pandemic has accelerated SCOs efforts to develop a joint response. During the third meeting of health ministers of the SCO member states on 24 July 2020, it was agreed to establish a coordination council and mechanism to jointly counteract disease outbreaks in the SCO space and assist member states in developing and implementing comprehensive measures in preventing, early reporting, responding, and mitigating the impact of diseases.

Source: *Shanghai Cooperation Organization.* SCO Health Ministers Advocate Combining Efforts of SCO Member States to Combat COVID-19 Pandemic. http://eng.sectsco.org/news/20200725/665852.html.

---

[62]   For instance, the Mekong Basin Disease Surveillance Program (MBDSP) is supported with policy and goodwill but resources are inadequate.

thus lowering the risk of them crossing. borders. Nonetheless, as the COVID-19 pandemic demonstrates, national efforts alone are insufficient to contain and manage emerging infectious diseases.

(iv) Regional IHR coordination and cooperation may have high political commitment, but also requires sufficient staff and funding.

86. Within the CAREC region, specific interventions and points of communication, coordination, cooperation, and collaboration would have to be assessed and discussed. A first step to advance collaboration is the establishment of a regional mechanism for knowledge sharing and dialogue. Such an approach has also been used for the GMS where a working group on health cooperation was established.[63] In addition, a project supports advancing RHS (Box 3). It is low in risk and intensity and may bring significant benefits in terms of leverage, capacity building, and technology transfer, which further contributes to saving costs and averting epidemic threats. The GMS project also aims to address gaps in RHS that are both national and regional priorities, such as surveillance and response, laboratory services, in-service training, and the control of other infectious diseases of regional relevance for which there was less funding.

Box 3: Greater Mekong Subregion Health Security Project

The GMS Health Security Project (a $114 million ADB loan) is a regional health security project that aims to improve regional cooperation and communicable disease control in border areas, strengthen national disease surveillance and outbreak response systems, and enhance laboratory services and hospital infection prevention and control.

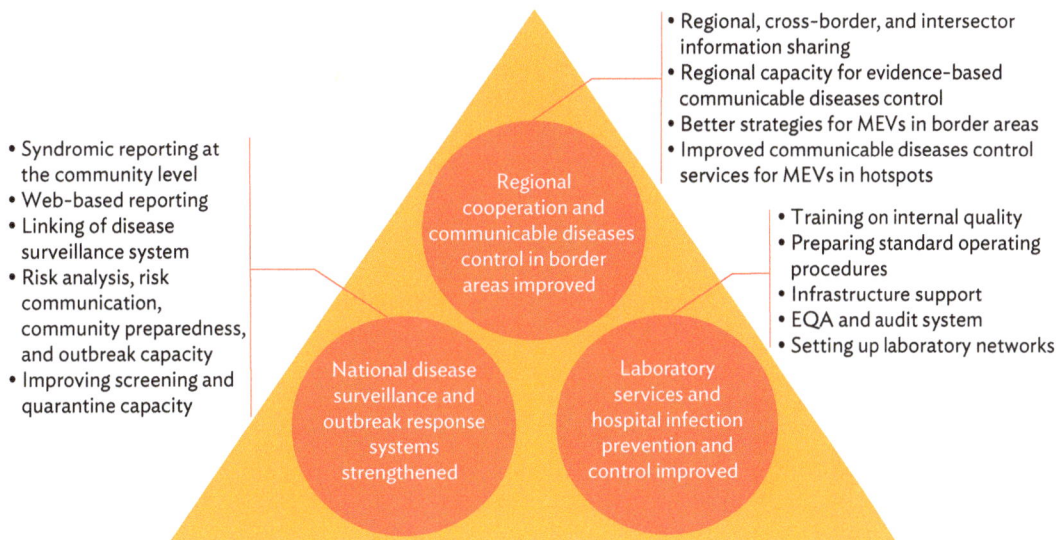

- Syndromic reporting at the community level
- Web-based reporting
- Linking of disease surveillance system
- Risk analysis, risk communication, community preparedness, and outbreak capacity
- Improving screening and quarantine capacity

Regional cooperation and communicable diseases control in border areas improved

- Regional, cross-border, and intersector information sharing
- Regional capacity for evidence-based communicable diseases control
- Better strategies for MEVs in border areas
- Improved communicable diseases control services for MEVs in hotspots

National disease surveillance and outbreak response systems strengthened

Laboratory services and hospital infection prevention and control improved

- Training on internal quality
- Preparing standard operating procedures
- Infrastructure support
- EQA and audit system
- Setting up laboratory networks

ADB = Asian Development Bank , EQA = external quality assessment, GMS = Greater Mekong Subregion, MEV = measles virus.
Source: ADB. Greater Mekong Subregion Health Security Project. https://www.adb.org/projects/48118-002/main.

---

63 Greater Mekong Subregion. Working Group on Health Cooperation. https://www.greatermekong.org/wghc.

Zoonoses and the One Health Approach

87.   Zoonoses are an RHS priority because of the impact these diseases have on public health, animal production, AMR, and food safety and security.[64] The One Health concept was introduced in the early 2000s. It brings together the human, animal, and plant health sectors and binds them to the ecosystems in which they exist. It is a collaborative, multidisciplinary, and multisector approach that can address urgent, ongoing, or potential health threats at human–animal–environment interface at subnational, national, regional, and global levels. The One Health approach is generally considered more efficient than other preventive measures; and multiple CAREC countries have implemented it (Box 4). International and national agencies have adopted this approach to tackle AMR.

88.   Based on e-SPAR self-assessment, countries in the region rate themselves quite high in terms of the One Health approach. In all CAREC countries, a coordination mechanism between the sectors is in place, and is usually activated when there is an acute threat such as the avian influenza epidemic. Surveillance of zoonoses has also been strengthened respectively among Afghanistan, Pakistan, and Turkmenistan.[65] Laboratory capacity to detect priority zoonotic diseases exists at both the human and animal health laboratories at the central level in all CAREC countries. The central veterinary laboratories have the capacity to detect several diseases and conduct vaccine effectiveness studies in livestock. However, further measures have to be taken beyond surveillance to improve the biosecurity of livestock.

Box 4: The One Health Approach in CAREC

In an effort to further improve the surveillance and management of the human, animal, plant, and environmental health, several Central Asia Regional Economic Cooperation (CAREC) Program countries adopted the One Health approach. For example, One Health surveillance in medical, veterinary, and environmental sectors in Kazakhstan has been improved with the use of the Electronic Integrated Disease Surveillance System (EIDSS). In 2016, EIDSS was deployed in Kazakhstan at 150 sites (271 sites planned) for veterinary surveillance and at 8 sites (23 sites planned) for human surveillance. Kazakhstan used EIDSS to develop a real-time control approach for the Crimean–Congo Hemorrhagic Fever. It provided a one-step tool for epidemiologists to make evidence-based decisions and plan response measures. EIDSS is already used in Azerbaijan and Georgia. Georgia's EIDSS and modern countrywide laboratory network, including the Lugar Center, was established based on the One Health approach. EIDSS has also been connected to the nationwide, unified Health Management Information System called "e-Health."

EIDSS presents an integrated solution that allows collecting, sharing, and analyzing data across sectors. This system has been implemented both for human and veterinary surveillance in Azerbaijan, Georgia, and Kazakhstan. In these countries, EIDSS provides a unique opportunity to improve monitoring and control capability to support the implementation of the One Health operational framework. The system can be further expanded to introduce methods for surveillance and control of brucellosis and other infectious diseases of special relevance in Central Asia and the Caucasus region, and other countries in CAREC.

Source: Authors based on: A. V. Burdakov, A. O. Ukharov, and T. G. Wahl. 2013. One Health Surveillance with Electronic Integrated Disease Surveillance System. *Online Journal of Public Health Information.* 5 (1). e199.

---

[64]   WHO. One Health. http://www.who.int/features/qa/one-health/en/.

[65]   One Health Network South Asia. Afghan One Health Hub. http://www.onehealthnetwork.asia/sites/afghanistanonehealthhub.

Food Safety

89.   Food safety is an IHR technical area with considerable variation among countries, which may cause transboundary outbreaks, long-term negative health impact, and economic losses. CAREC countries have appreciated this as a regional priority. The CAREC Program supports modernization of sanitary and phytosanitary (SPS) systems to ensure food safety, animal health, and plant health for regional trade under the CAREC framework (Box 5).

Laboratory Services

90.   High quality and efficient laboratory services are an essential cornerstone of RHS to track diseases and investigate events. The laboratory capacities within and among countries is very mixed, with some reference laboratories not meeting international standards. WHO Regional Office for Europe has been leading a program to upgrade laboratory services (Box 6). Since COVID-19, upgrading has accelerated with major investments in staff training, infrastructure,

---

Box 5: Modernization of Sanitary and Phytosanitary Standards in Countries

Since 2011, Central Asia Regional Economic Cooperation (CAREC) Program countries have been undertaking assessments to improve sanitary and phytosanitary standards (SPS) capacities as part of trade facilitation initiatives under CAREC.[a] In 2015, CAREC ministers endorsed the Common Agenda for Modernization of SPS Measures for Trade (CAST), a regional framework for priority actions to upgrade SPS measures and complement customs-related initiatives in the CAREC region.[b] Under the CAREC 2030 strategy, the alignment of SPS measures with international standards remains a priority.[c] The strategy promotes regional cooperation to facilitate trade, and agriculture trade expansion through agriculture value chains—while controlling transboundary pests and animal diseases and developing a food safety network. The CAREC Integrated Trade Agenda 2030 supports the implementation of CAST through establishment of a CAREC-wide SPS working group.

Between 2003 and 2019, ADB financed 8 investment and 12 technical assistance projects to help CAREC developing member countries align food safety, animal health, and plant health with the World Trade Organization's SPS Agreement.[d] An investment project in the People's Republic of China aimed to improve livestock safety monitoring and inspection system at production and processing stages, enhance food safety control, and implement environmentally sustainable livestock industry.[e] A project in Mongolia supported the upgrading of laboratories and inspection facilities for animal health, strengthening inspection management systems, and aligning SPS controls and inspections with international standards.[f]

[a] ADB. 2014. *CAREC Transport and Trade Facilitation Strategy 2020.* Manila.
[b] R. Black. 2018. Progress on CAREC Common Agenda for Modernization of SPS Measures for Trade (CAST). Presentation at the Inaugural Meeting of the CAREC Regional Trade Group. Bangkok. 25-26 June. https://www.carecprogram.org/uploads/11-Progress-on-CAST-by-Mr.-Rob-Black.pdf.
[c] ADB. 2017 *CAREC 2030: Connecting the Region for Shared and Sustainable Development.* Manila.
[d] ADB. 2019. *Modernizing Sanitary and Phytosanitary Measures in CAREC: An Assessment and the Way Forward.* Manila: ADB-CAREC.
[e] ADB. 2015. *Henan Sustainable Livestock Farming and Product Safety Demonstration Project.* Manila.
[f] ADB. 2015. *Regional Upgrades of Sanitary and Phytosanitary Measures for Trade Project.* Manila.
Source: Author's summary.

Box 6: Strengthening National Quality Assurance Systems and Laboratory Capacity in CAREC Countries

Among the Central Asia Regional Economic Cooperation (CAREC) Program countries, Kazakhstan has developed a national quality assurance system and laboratory services. It has also introduced capacity building activities and a mentoring program to assure compliance with international approaches in laboratory accreditation and quality assurance of laboratory practices. In the Kyrgyz Republic, health authorities are establishing national standards for laboratory certification and a quality management system for laboratory research. They are also introducing a mentoring program for laboratories. To address human resource development needs, the Kyrgyz Republic also evaluated and updated the national training curriculum for laboratory personnel. Pakistan has several laboratories with excellent capabilities, some of which are accredited by the International Organization for Standardization (ISO).[a] The People's Republic of China (PRC) has some of the most advanced laboratory capacities and network in the region.[b] While laboratory licensing is generally applied in the CAREC countries, laboratory standards remain poorly regulated and reinforced. Both public and private laboratory services require major capacity building in terms on quality and biosafety. Since 2012, the World Health Organization (WHO) Europe and partners have worked together on the *Better Labs for Better Health* initiative to strengthen laboratory services.[c] The coronavirus disease (COVID-19) funding also provides an opportunity for further strengthening of laboratory services.

[a] Eight laboratories are accredited by the Pakistan National Accreditation Council to ISO standards. Transportation of samples within Pakistan is also well-managed. WHO. 2017. *Joint External Evaluation of IHR Core Capacities of the Islamic Republic of Pakistan*. Geneva.

[b] WHO Regional Office for Europe, 2018. UHC and SDG Country Profile 2018: China.

[c] WHO. 2012. Better Labs for Better Health. Strengthening Laboratory Systems in the WHO European Region. Report of the 3rd Partners Meeting with a focus on Antimicrobial Resistance. Kazakhstan. https://www.euro.who.int/__data/assets/pdf_file/0003/400296/Partners-Meeting-2018-Report-en.pdf.

Source: Author.

---

equipment, and supplies, essentially to scale up COVID-19 testing capacity. The focus is currently on molecular diagnostics for virology and some related clinical tests. However, the laboratory services require much broader upgrading and quality improvement, networking, and at least functional integration of services, which will benefit both national health services and RHS.

Surveillance and Response

91.   RHS depends on rapid detection of public health risks through syndromic reporting, and the prompt investigation, risk assessment, notification, and response to these risks. To this end, a sensitive and flexible surveillance system with an early warning function is required. Mongolia and the PRC have been reported as having excellent surveillance (and investigative response), while other CAREC countries have the potential to improve in these areas. Since COVID-19, major investments have been made to strengthen physical surveillance capacity. Only the PRC has a full real-time digital monitoring system. Efforts are being made in CAREC countries to develop the national and regional capacity to analyze and link data through the national surveillance systems, as well as to ensure intersector collaboration between human, animal, and plant health sectors (Box 4). Capability to rapidly collect and analyze information from these sectors is challenging due to different systems often used in these areas.[66]

---

[66]   A. V. Burdakov, A. O. Ukharov, and T. G. Wahl. 2013. One Health Surveillance with Electronic Integrated Disease Surveillance System. *Online Journal of Public Health Information*. 5 (1). e199.

92. ICT-related technologies and tools have a role to play in ensuring health security. Examples of these are geospatial technologies, digital diagnostic equipment and laboratory information systems, mobile applications (for disease surveillance and reporting), and electronic health records (that can identify patients wherever and whenever they interact with the health system while ensuring patient privacy), and harmonization of terminology and data standards across borders. Recent outbreaks, particularly the COVID-19, and the treatment of COVID-19 patients (e.g., virtual consultation) have demonstrated that investments should go beyond traditional communicable diseases surveillance systems and build strong foundations for digitally enabled information systems, which place patients at the center.

93. The existing Electronic Integrated Disease Surveillance System (EIDSS) can be further developed for expanded application at the regional level. CAREC can support the initiative by facilitating the development of regional standards for data content and exchange, and regional collaboration in identifying and responding to data security threats, and fostering a common approach to health data governance that include multiple countries. One direction for CAREC could be to establish a regional network of surveillance and burden assessment. Such a network would benefit from cross-country learning and information sharing. Economies of scale can also be achieved from implementing a range of similar surveys, and from collective bargaining with institutions that conduct such surveys.

94. CAREC countries have also undertaken significant efforts to strengthen regional response to infectious and zoonotic diseases (Box 7).

95. There are several subregional CAREC initiatives that aim to strengthen collaboration on infectious diseases surveillance. For example, there is an electronic HIV case management system used by multiple CAREC country AIDS centers, primarily in Kazakhstan, the Kyrgyz Republic, and Tajikistan, to provide reliable real-time data on HIV epidemics. Georgia and Pakistan have established viral hepatitis centers that could serve as regional hubs.

96. CAREC countries, with support from ADB, are working together to improve regulatory alignment and strengthen laboratory capacity and border services management in line with the World Trade Organization Agreement on the Application of SPS Measures (Box 5). While the current SPS modernization efforts in CAREC focus mostly on animal, plant health, and food safety, they can be expanded to include human health. Adding human health components would allow for significant efficiency gains and sustainability.

97. For emerging and re-emerging infectious diseases, real-time surveillance and the ability to collect and test (human and animal) samples rapidly and precisely are essential to identify disease outbreaks. National and regional reporting systems and qualified human resources for response should also support the control of outbreaks. Since surveillance, diagnosis, and control of zoonotic disease take place at the interface between animals and humans, systematic communication and substantial coordination between human, wildlife, and veterinary health services are vital. The GMS Health Security Project provides a comprehensive case on how various aspects of health interventions are addressed for subregional health security (Box 3). In view of current regional health threats and ongoing RHS investment in the CAREC region, developing regional real-time surveillance and response system including the One Health approach and SPS modernization, coupled with increased information exchange and diagnostic capacity, can be a good entry point for strengthening RHS.

Box 7: Regional Cooperation and Surveillance of Infectious Diseases in Countries

Among the Central Asia Regional Economic Cooperation (CAREC) Program countries, the People's Republic of China (PRC) hosts one of the six World Health Organization (WHO) Collaborating Centers on Influenza[a] under the Global Influenza Surveillance and Response System in improving surveillance, preparedness, and response for seasonal, pandemic, and zoonotic influenza. The PRC's Health Silk Road (HSR) program promotes cooperation among participating countries in broad areas, such as prevention and control of communicable diseases, improving medical system and policies, health care capacity building, staff training and exchange, traditional medicine, health education, disaster relief, aid, and poverty reduction.[b] In 2017, the PRC signed a Memorandum of Understanding with WHO, which aims to promote global health security and development.[c]

Kazakhstan hosts the Global Disease Detection Regional Center (GDDRC), 1 of the 10 worldwide centers that help countries identify and respond to emerging diseases.[d] The GDDRC Regional Center collaborates with key partners in Kazakhstan, the Kyrgyz Republic, Tajikistan, Turkmenistan, and Uzbekistan, and works with the WHO and ministries of health of participating countries to strengthen core infrastructures (e.g., laboratory detection, clinical surveillance, outbreak investigation and control) to comply with the International Health Regulations. In 2017, the Kyrgyz Republic and Tajikistan worked on creating a single approach and system for transporting samples between laboratories.[e]

In collaboration with the United States Centers for Disease Control and Prevention (CDC), Georgia is transforming its state-of-the-art national reference laboratory, the Lugar Center, into a Center of Excellence in the Caucasus region.[f] In collaboration with the WHO, Georgia is investing in infrastructure to create a regional laboratory that will make the country and the region a diagnostic leader in identifying and preventing antimicrobial resistance. The Lugar Center would serve approximately 17 million people in the South Caucasus region (Armenia, Azerbaijan, and Georgia).

[a] WHO. WHO Collaborating Centres for Influenza and their Terms of Reference. https://www.who.int/influenza/gisrs_laboratory/collaborating_centres/list/en/.

[b] K. Tang et al. 2017. China's Silk Road and Global Health. *The Lancet*. 390 (10112). pp. 2595–2601.

[c] *WHO Media Centre*. China and WHO Adopt Transformative Approach: Linking Health and Economic Development with New Agreement on One Belt One Road Initiative. 29 January. http://www.wpro.who.int/china/mediacentre/releases/2017/20170119-mr-president-xi-visit-to-WHO-HQ/en/.

[d] CDC. 2017. Factsheet on *CDC in Kazakhstan*. https://www.cdc.gov/globalhealth/countries/kazakhstan/pdf/kazakhstan_factsheet.pdf.

[e] WHO. Better Labs as a Bridge to Stronger Health System in Kyrgyz Republic. https://www.euro.who.int/en/countries/kyrgyzstan/areas-of-work/better-labs-as-a-bridge-to-a-stronger-health-system-in-kyrgyzstan.

[f] CDC. 2016. Combatting AMR/HAI in South Caucasus. Global Health – Stories. 14 July. https://www.cdc.gov/globalhealth/stories/combatting_amr_hai_caucasus.html.

Source: Author's summary based on related literature and J. Chen et al. 2019. Combating Infectious Disease Epidemics through China's Belt and Road Initiative. *PLOS Neglected Tropical Diseases* 13 (4). e0007107. https://doi.org/10.1371/journal.pntd.0007107.

Human Resources for Regional Health Security

98.   Human resources development is a priority for RHS. With the exception of the PRC, most of the CAREC countries have not yet adequately met human resource requirements for IHR. The appropriate human resource mix of competencies, including knowledge and skills, is critical to sustaining public health surveillance and responding to regional health threats. Investment in training and research and development (R&D) at the regional level can lead to efficiency gains and economies of scale, since small countries may not have the resources to invest in human resources training on EIDs. Since such diseases tend to be new, unpredictable and sometimes rare, countries may also not be able to prioritize and allocate enough resources for R&D. The WHO and other partners have been supporting capacity building for surveillance and response, including

training programs for laboratory services, field epidemiology, and infection prevention and control. Several CAREC countries are currently building the capacity of public health professionals through a variety of regional learning solutions, including training activities, materials, and tools (Box 8).

National Health Emergency Framework

99.   During the COVID-19 pandemic, CAREC countries have demonstrated sound national health emergency frameworks and partnerships. The governments exercised good leadership with support of the United Nations Development Programme, and health ministries worked closely together with WHO and other partners. It is hoped that this multisector and interagency collaboration will be sustained after the COVID-19 pandemic and continue to help achieve the SDGs and health for all by all.

Box 8: Regional Human Resources Training in CAREC Countries

The Training Programs in Epidemiology and Public Health Interventions Network (TEPHINET) is a professional network of 73 field epidemiology training programs, including those with laboratory and veterinary components, working across more than 100 countries.[a] TEPHINET supports the Central Asia Field Epidemiology and Laboratory Training Program (FELTP). FELTP focuses on applied epidemiology, disease surveillance, outbreak response, laboratory methods, and program evaluation with additional courses in study design and scientific writing. While enrolled, residents continue working in their respective countries' health systems, and are well-positioned to serve as first responders to outbreaks and as leaders and mentors for future in-country specialists in field epidemiology. The FELTP residents and graduates participate in AMR and hospital-acquired infections (HAI) surveillance programs. FELTP has been implemented in Afghanistan, Azerbaijan, Georgia, Kazakhstan, the Kyrgyz Republic, Pakistan, Ukraine, and Uzbekistan.[b] The FELTP in Pakistan, based in the National Institute of Health, served as a key technical arm during public health threats, including the human avian influenza outbreak in 2007, an HIV outbreak in 2008, the flood response in 2010, and the dengue outbreak in 2011. FELTP also established several hepatitis surveillance sites in Pakistan.[c]

CAREC = Central Asia Regional Economic Program.

[a] TEPHINET. https://www.tephinet.org.

[b] South Caucasus Field Epidemiology and Training Program. https://www.tephinet.org/training-programs/south-caucasus-field-epidemiology-and-laboratory-training-program.

[c] Government of Pakistan, National Institute of Health. Field Epidemiology and Laboratory Training Program. https://www.nih.org.pk/field-epidemiology-laboratory-training-program-feltp-2/.

Source: Author's summary.

Health Service Provision

100.　Health service provision, especially hospital surge capacity for quarantine services and intensive care treatment, was clearly insufficient in the CAREC region and elsewhere during the COVID-19 pandemic. While it is unrealistic to expect countries to maintain full surge capacity for a major pandemic, even a modest surge was hard to handle because of lack of facilities and trained staff. The COVID-19 pandemic has triggered major investment in increasing quarantine facilities and intensive care capacity. Bringing human resources will take much longer and should be prioritized. Post-COVID-19 planning will require guidance on how to apply, operate, and maintain these investments and improve health system resilience.

101.　As part of quality improvement of hospital services, infection prevention and control (IPC) is a technical area that is generally substandard in many hospitals due to lack of maintenance, equipment, and medical waste management. The WHO has initiated a global IPC program but implementation has been slow due to capacity and financing constraints. COVID-19 has triggered investments to quickly improve the larger hospitals handling COVID-19 patients, but further management strengthening, human resources development, and facility upgrading will be required to address the current IPC situation.

Risk Communication

102.　Risk communication for public health threats and other emergencies is led by the government with support of various agencies, businesses, and key partners such as the WHO. Risk communication for the COVID-19 pandemic in CAREC countries is yet to be assessed, but consultations suggest that it was substantial and effective. Most governments were quick to fully inform the public about the pending pandemic and subsequent control measures using mass media, state and religious institutions, grassroot organizations, and social media. For the most part, the general public demonstrated acceptance of lockdown measures and a high level of compliance with social distancing and use of face masks and disinfectants that may be attributed to the legacy of the Soviet Union with its emphasis on sanitary measures. [67]

Points of Entry

103.　As per IHR (2005), points of entry are an essential part of the country's surveillance system to minimize the risk of the spread of infectious diseases between countries. CAREC countries have designated major international airports, ports and land crossing as point of entry (POE) to maintain public sanitation and vector control, conduct risk communication, screen persons and goods on entry, and provide quarantine and other control measures as needed. CAREC countries also share many border crossings for local travel without POE services. A large number of people and goods pass the borders each day. With the current technology, it is not possible to screen all persons and goods except for the most basic questioning and inspection. Screening for infectious cases at POE has a very low yield. Typically, infectious patients will get sick after crossing the border and are diagnosed in a clinic or hospital. Surveillance of people and goods moving across borders has to be initiated at the starting point (at home or in the farm or factory) and followed to the end-point of each journey (at home or hospital, market or shop using tools such as instructions, self-assessment, rapid test, inspection, and certification. Surveillance systems registering travel of people and goods may be digitally linked across borders while at the same time ensuring protection of privacy and protecting vulnerable groups.

---

[67]　Several studies suggest variance in compliance to social distancing may have cultural or historical origins. However, more research into this relationship is needed. UNCTAD. 2020. *Coronagraben: Culture and Social Distancing in Times of COVID-19.* https://unctad.org/system/files/official-document/ser-rp-2020d8_en.pdf.

Chemical and Radiation Events

104.   CAREC countries, except Afghanistan, report high IHR performance for chemical and radiation events.[68] However, several CAREC countries depend on expertise from other countries to handle such events. The JEE brings professionals to update the situation in each country, which is technically quite complex.

Control of other Diseases of Regional Relevance

105.   HIV/AIDS poses real regional health threats in connection to changing lifestyle and substance abuse. Bilateral collaboration has been ongoing to help contain this threat. In the CAREC region, tuberculosis is another major regional health threat due to a very high level of multidrug resistance TB and large cost implications, among others. Given the global dimensions of this multidrug resistance threat, partners are currently assisting various countries to strengthen diagnostic and treatment capacities. CAREC cooperation could add a regional control dimension to that, including for migrant health workers. Other infectious diseases of regional relevance such as zoonoses, dengue, and malaria need to be more closely examined in terms of their regional impact.

Supporting Health Systems Development through Regional Cooperation

106.   From the national health systems perspective, NCDs and their risk factors put major strains on services delivery and stretch health sector budgets. They are likely to increase the health sector's burden in the future with population aging, lifestyle changes, and demand for medical technologies. This foremost requires a multisector approach, especially in dealing with lifestyle change and care for the elderly. The health sector has to be restructured to become more effective and efficient in the prevention and treatment of NCDs, communicable diseases (CDs), accidents and injuries, and in maternal and child health and nutrition. This requires better health infrastructure; adequate human resources; and access to medicines, medical technologies, and quality of care. Health governance, financing, and insurance systems have to be improved. The COVID-19 pandemic has likely resulted in major and long-lasting impact on regular health services that have to be adjusted during the post-COVID-19 health sector planning toward SDGs.[69] This analysis suggests RHC to build resilient health systems that aim to improve quality and efficiency of health services and address the national burden of diseases. While the following analysis focuses on NCDs, building strong health systems is equally important for controlling CDs and improving maternal and child health.

107.   Services for NCDs are generally considered more of a national than a regional health priority. However, there are strong rationales for regional cooperation in NCDs because of potential mutual benefits for CAREC countries. From the COVID-19 pandemic experience, reducing the burden of NCDs will minimize the spread and impact of EIDs. It will also reduce high out-of-pocket spending associated with chronic NCDs that are likely to weigh more heavily on low income groups. Regional technology transfer and

---

[68]   Chemical events and radiation emergencies are two separate capacities in the e-SPAR of the IHR.

[69]   T. Roberton et al. 2020. Early Estimates of the Indirect Effects of the COVID-19 Pandemic on Maternal and Child Mortality in Low-Income and Middle-Income Countries: A Modelling Study. *The Lancet Global Health.* 8 (7). 12 May. e901–908. Maryland: Johns Hopkins University. https://www.thelancet.com/journals/langlo/article/PIIS2214-109X(20)30229-1/fulltext.

capacity building in NCD services can achieve better prevention and treatment of NCDs. Joint action can mobilize resources and improve efficiency in controlling NCDs. Developing regional standards can also contribute to reducing CDs and NCDs, for example, through quality control of medicines and food products and harmonized taxation policies on "sin goods."

108.   Regional interventions can be actualized to prevent or reduce the NCD burden. Cost-effective interventions that address cardiovascular disease (CVD), tobacco use, alcohol abuse, consumption of unhealthy fats, and excessive salt intake are now better understood. Evidence shows that both population-based (e.g., tobacco measures and a reduction in salt intake) and individual-based interventions (e.g., drugs to prevent or manage CVD by reducing blood pressure or cholesterol) are effective at reducing the NCD burden. Both types of interventions lend themselves to regional cooperation within CAREC. Some policy options and actions address NCD-specific risk factors and conditions and will require strong multisector action; while some strategies are broader and target health building blocks in the wider health system to strengthen the overall NCD response.

Multisector Action to Tackle Noncommunicable Diseases: Harmonizing Tax Policies and Food Labeling

109.   Harmonizing health policies and strategies at regional level enhances NCD prevention and control efforts, especially for tobacco, alcohol, and food. This can lead to capacity building, technology transfer, economies of scale, and efficiency gains. The most cost-effective policy tool for tobacco control is taxation of tobacco products, which has been highly effective in reducing the prevalence of smoking in both developed and developing countries.[70] WHO Framework Convention on Tobacco Control (FCTC) signatories (all CAREC countries) are committed to levying excise taxes on tobacco products. Tax policies on tobacco products vary widely across CAREC countries. These regional strategies should go hand in hand with strengthening tobacco anti-smuggling measures. Smuggling, if unchecked, may undermine advertising and tax policies designed to reduce demand and consumption. Box 9 demonstrates the implementation of WHO FCTC in the CAREC region.

110.   Another regional approach targeting NCD risk factors can be the standardization of food labeling policies across the region. Such policies lead to stronger negotiating position for countries relative to the food industry, as well as economies of scale, by applying same labels among several countries. Regional food labeling can also assist national efforts in mitigating the growing problem of obesity, through increasing awareness of calorie content (complement awareness campaigns for healthy foods) and contribute to hypertension control efforts by reducing salt intake.

Information Systems

111.   Cross-border collaboration for health care services through information sharing and improved surveillance is nothing new, with more

---

[70]   P. Jha and F. Chaloupka. 2006. *Tobacco Control in Developing Countries*. Washington, DC.: World Bank.

Box 9: Implementation of WHO Framework Convention on Tobacco Control in CAREC Countries

All Central Asia Regional Economic Cooperation (CAREC) Program countries are signatories to the World Health Organization Framework Convention on Tobacco Control (WHO FCTC). The WHO recommended tobacco tax rate is 70%. Pakistan has a complex three-tier tax system, which indirectly supports cigarette production and consumption, [a] and the WHO has called upon the country to increase tobacco taxation (currently at 60.3%) to 70%. Pakistan may be facing annual revenue losses of Rs30 billion (approximately $193.37 million) due to low taxes on the tobacco industry, while the health of the nation's youth is at stake.

Compared to the region, tobacco tax in Afghanistan is low at around 34%. Tobacco imports in Afghanistan are estimated to be higher than domestic consumption. Available data indicate that approximately 76% of imported cigarettes are consumed by the Afghan population, and 24% are re-exported. [b]

In 2019, Azerbaijan increased tobacco excise taxes, but such taxes were also increased in Armenia, Georgia, and the Russian Federation; therefore, the tax burden in Azerbaijan is still much lower than in neighboring countries. According to the World Bank, "Tobacco industry tries to exaggerate the problem of cigarette smuggling into Azerbaijan to create an impression that tobacco taxes should not be increased, as smuggling is already very high. However, cigarette smuggling into Azerbaijan is not caused by differences in tax rates, as the tobacco excise burden in Azerbaijan is much lower. Relatively high prices in Azerbaijan are mainly determined by the pricing policy of the tobacco industry. However, over recent years, cigarettes in Azerbaijan were cheaper than in [the Russian Federation] so numerous cases of cigarette smuggling from Azerbaijan to [the Russian Federation] were registered." [c]

[a] D. Nayab et al. 2018. *Economics of Tobacco Taxation and Consumption in Pakistan.* Islamabad: Pakistan Institute of Development Economics.
[b] A.C. Medici et al. 2018. Options for Tobacco Taxation in Afghanistan. *Knowledge Brief.* Washington DC: World Bank Group.
[c] World Bank. 2019. Azerbaijan: Overview of Tobacco Use, Tobacco Control, Legislation and Taxation, Global Tobacco Control Program. Country Brief. Geneva.
Source: Author's summary.

---

than 50 years in cancer research.[71] With the rapid advance in digital technology, collaboration across countries to pool data and resources becomes more possible and beneficial. It has great potential in tapping the unprecedented capacity for data storage and processing to advance scientific research, increasing the accuracy of diagnoses and the effectiveness of treatment, as well as improving policies that benefit patients and societies. This is particularly useful for rare health conditions. Combining datasets increases sample sizes, which yield more reliable statistical results and increase the ability of research to detect rare events—as any single country would not have sufficient resources for such research on their own.

---

[71] The International Agency for Research on Cancer (IARC) was launched in 1965. It publishes comparable indicators of cancer incidence and mortality. International Agency for Research on Cancer. 2019. *Biennial Report 2018–2019.* Lyon, France. https://publications.iarc.fr/Book-And-Report-Series/Iarc-Biennial-Reports/IARC-Biennial-Report-2018-2019.

The European Cancer Information System (ECIS) provides indicators of cancer incidence, mortality and survival, and the EUROCARE study provides indicators of 5-year relative survival. ECIS. 2019. *European Cancer Information System.* https://ecis.jrc.ec.europa.eu/ (accessed July 2019); EUROCARE. 2019. *EUROCARE - Survival of Cancer Patients In Europe.* http://www.eurocare.it/ (accessed July 2019).

The RARECAREnet study, using data from EUROCARE-5, reported comparable indicators of cancer incidence, prevalence, and survival of rare types of cancer. RARECARENET. 2019. *Information Network on Rare Cancers.* http://www.rarecarenet.eu/ (accessed July 2019).

Box 10 provides an example of cooperation among Nordic countries on NCD surveillance and research.

112.   Data must be valid and comparable to have reliable results. This requires adherence to shared data standards and definitions, and interoperability. Some of the biggest barriers to stronger cooperation include the lack of common data standards and terminology for information exchange, local legislation and regulation, and data privacy concerns. These are also common barriers to sharing and diffusing data-driven technologies among health care organizations across countries. In addressing NCDs, CAREC countries have already employed various approaches to keep pace with the latest health technologies while maintaining affordable access to health care for patients.[72]

113.   Information systems that can collect sex-disaggregated data are important in monitoring progress on key health outcomes that could also be monitored at regional level. Some risk factors for NCDs and major causes of morbidity and mortality are being localized and tracked as part of SDG indicators. However, national health information systems remain fragmented in the CAREC region, and are not always well-linked to information systems for human resources, supplies, and finance—making it difficult to link SDG indicators with resources. The United Nations is in the process of assisting countries to align resources with SDG indicators.[73] ADB and the WHO have further supported the development of a UHC monitoring framework that links inputs to outcome, and impact indicators that could be applied at local and regional levels.[74]

Box 10: Regional Cooperation on Noncommunicable Disease Surveillance and Research in Nordic Countries

The Nordic Council of Ministers (Denmark, Finland, Iceland, Norway, and Sweden) established NordForsk in 2005 to strengthen Nordic research across scientific domains and the Nordic Programme on Health and Welfare.[a] The program aims to increase public health and welfare in the Nordic countries through multidisciplinary research. It involves investments in high quality information infrastructure, including harmonization of population-based registries and biobanks of participating countries to link their data for analysis.

By pooling data from health registries in Demark, Finland, Norway, and Sweden with data from the UK Clinical Practice Research Datalink, a multinational sample was created allowing the study of cancer incidence among new insulin users. Data pooling resulted in 21,000 cases of cancer that could be studied over a follow-up period of about 5 years and enabled examining the risk of developing 10 types of cancer.[b]

[a] NordForsk. Nordic Programme on Health and Welfare. https://www.nordforsk.org/programs/nordic-programme-health-and-welfare.

[b] A. But et al. 2017. Cancer Risk Among Insulin Users: Comparing Analogues With Human Insulin in the CARING Five-Country Cohort Study. *Diabetologia*. 60. pp. 1691–1703. http://dx.doi.org/10.1007/s00125-017-4312-5.

Source: Author's summary.

---

[72]   Health technology in its broadest context includes pharmaceuticals, vaccines, medical devices, medical and surgical procedures, and the systems within which health is protected and maintained.

[73]   United Nations. 2019. *United Nations Secretary General's Roadmap for Financing the 2030 Agenda for Sustainable Development. 2019–2021* New York.

[74]   ADB. 2016. *Monitoring Universal Health Coverage in the Western Pacific: Framework, Indicators, and Dashboard.* Manila. https://www.adb.org/publications/monitoring-universal-health-coverage-western-pacific.

Human Resources for Health

114.   Health professionals are central to the prevention and treatment of patients with NCDs, yet most CAREC countries are facing a shortage of highly qualified health professionals, especially in rural areas. There is considerable migration of health professionals within and outside the CAREC region. Migrant labor statistics in the region are not sufficiently disaggregated (by profession) to form a clear estimate of the number of health professionals that have migrated, however, trends can be extrapolated from existing statistical evidence.[75] The Russian Federation has been attracting health workers from other former Soviet Union republics,[76] since medical qualifications are mutually recognized and there is no language barrier. Professional mobility between Kazakhstan, the Kyrgyz Republic, and the Russian Federation has been further facilitated by the Eurasian Customs Union, which allows for the free movement of labor between these countries.[77]

115.   Labor, training, and migration of health professionals could be addressed from a regional perspective. For countries that are small or resource-constrained, regional training of health professionals (e.g., through a regional center of excellence) would offer benefits such as lower costs and higher-quality education in settings with greater clinical expertise and adequate caseload for training. Currently, many CAREC countries' health students are studying in the PRC, with few regulated regional programs in place.

116.   Aligning data sources and sharing information of migrant health workers in the CAREC region can facilitate the hiring of migrant health professionals in the receiving or employing countries. This can be done through establishing regional migrant registries and databases, and connecting them to a database of prospective employers in the health sector. A further challenge lies in the mismatch of medical skills of migrant health professionals in the receiving or employing countries. For example, Central Asian health migrants to the Russian Federation tend to work in jobs below their skill levels. Migrants are also more difficult to find suitable jobs in the health sector, comparing with migrants with working experience in other sectors.[78]

117.   According to the International Labour Organization (ILO), a similar strategy to address "brain drain" is based on the concept of circulation of skills, which requires enhanced cooperation between origin and destination countries, creating "win-win" for both countries.[79] Some initiatives include mentor–sponsor programs, joint research projects, peer review mechanisms, virtual return (through distance teaching and eLearning), and short-term visits and assignments.[80] In addition, the skills of the diasporas can be tapped by establishing

---

[75]   Certain professions could be more affected by migration. For example, health care and education, due to global demand, could lead to a failure in delivery of key social services in countries of origin. L. T. Katseli, R. E. Lucas, and T. Xenogiani. 2006. *Effects of Migration on Sending Countries*. Turin, Italy: OECD.

[76]   The international recruitment of health workers by countries outside the former Soviet Union is not a significant feature of most of the countries in the CAREC region.

[77]   E. Richardson et al. 2013. *Belarus: Health System Review, Health Systems in Transition*. 15 (5). pp. 1–118.

[78]   United Nations Development Programme Regional Bureau for Europe and the Commonwealth of Independent States. 2015. Labour Migration, Migration, Remittances, and Human Development in Central Asia. *Central Asia Human Development Series*. New York.

[79]   P. Wickramasekara. 2003. *Policy Response to Skilled Migration: Retention, Return and Circulation*. Geneva: International Migration Branch (MIGRANT) International Labour Organisation.

[80]   P. Wickramasekara. 2004. Rights of Migrant Workers in Asia: Any Light at the End of the Tunnel? *Social Protection Sector, International Migration Programme*. Geneva: International Labour Organization.

Box 11: Health Services under ASEAN Economic Community

The Association of Southeast Asian Nations (ASEAN) Economic Community (AEC) was established in 2015. The concept of a single market is based on the principles of free flow of trade in services and skilled labor. To facilitate intra-regional mobility of health professionals, two mutual recognition arrangements (MRAs) were set up, one for nursing (2006) and one for medicine and dentistry professionals (2009).

The ASEAN Coordinating Committee on Services set up the Healthcare Services Sectoral Working Group (HSSWG) to discuss cooperation in health care services and implementation of the ASEAN Framework Agreement on Services (AFAS). In addition to the MRAs, the agenda of the HSSWG meetings also include information exchanges; regional profiling and databases of professionals, institutions, infrastructures, and systems; domestic regulations; development of core competencies and equivalences; capacity building programs; formulation of yearly work programs; and other initiatives relevant to the AFAS implementation.[a] Implementation of the health-related MRAs is slow due to various factors. Greater political will is required to achieve the free flow of health workers in the ASEAN region.[b]

[a] ASEAN. Healthcare Services. https://asean.org/asean-economic-community/sectoral-bodies-under-the-purview-of-aem/services/healthcare-services/.
[b] T. Vannarath et al. 2018. The Impact of ASEAN Economic Integration on Health Worker Mobility: A Scoping Review of the Literature. *Health Policy and Planning* October. 33 (8). pp. 957–965.
Source: Association of Southeast Asian Nations. ASEAN Joint Coordinating Committee on Medical Practitioners. https://asean.org/asean-economic-community/sectoral-bodies-under-the-purview-of-aem/services/healthcare-services/medical-practitioners-ajccm/ (accessed 6 February 2020).

---

knowledge exchange networks.[81] A regional solution to address the "brain drain" issue is exemplified by mutual recognition agreements (MRAs), such as in the Association of Southeast Asian Nations (ASEAN) (Box 11).[82]

118.	Afghanistan, the Kyrgyz Republic, Pakistan, and Tajikistan have also been addressing the critical shortage of adequately skilled staff in hard-to-reach areas by using digital health solutions, such as telemedicine. Main barriers to accessing hospital and specialized services identified in several CAREC countries are geographical and financial. Geographical access is particularly a concern in countries with vast territories and low population densities (Mongolia and Kazakhstan) or those with mountainous terrains (Afghanistan, the Kyrgyz Republic, Tajikistan). Accessibility in rural areas is also a concern in providing emergency medicine. Rural areas are often disadvantaged in terms of life-saving equipment (including ambulance vehicles) and modern communication technologies. Regional training on eHealth can be an effective way to mitigate this constraint (Box 12).

---

[81]	The Kyrgyz Republic and Tajikistan are both using their diasporas living in the Russian Federation to support arriving migrants.

[82]	ASEAN. Medical Practitioners (AJCCM). https://asean.org/asean-economic-community/sectoral-bodies-under-the-purview-of-aem/services/healthcare-services/medical-practitioners-ajccm/.

Box 12: Regional Training and eHealth in CAREC

There are several regional efforts to alleviate insufficient qualified health personnel through eLearning[a] and telemedicine initiatives in CAREC. For example, a regional initiative supported by the Aga Khan Development Network (AKDN) introduced digital health connections both at the country level (urban–to–rural facilities in the Kyrgyz Republic and Tajikistan) and at the regional level from Tajikistan to Afghanistan and Pakistan for teleconsultations and eLearning sessions.[b] The Health services are provided in some of the very remote and mountainous areas, and some hospitals also use teleradiology services. Through eLearning initiatives, health care and community workers have improved access to training, data collection and analysis, and diagnostic and clinical decision-making support. Another initiative that has been implemented in several CAREC countries is the establishment of virtual communities of practice for health practitioners under Project ECHO (Extension for Community Healthcare Outcomes). The project facilitates case-based learning, peer–to–peer learning, and supervised practice, and provides access to online resources. The project is also being implemented at the regional level. Such projects can be further supported through applying information and communication technology (e.g., replicated and scaled) to increase the scope and countries involved, multiplying the benefits across CAREC borders.[c]

[a] eLearning refers to the use of electronic technology and media for training and education. It helps (i) improve the quality of education and increase access to learning in geographically isolated locations or of those with insufficient local training facilities, (ii) make health sciences education available to a broader audience and make better use of existing educational resources, (iii) achieve universal health coverage by improving the knowledge and skills of the health workforce, and (iv) increase the number of trained professionals with specialized or general skills.

[b] *United States Agency for International Development*. Can Telecommunications Bring Health Care to the Hard-to-Reach? https://medium.com/usaid-2030/can-telecommunications-bring-health-care-to-the-hard-to-reach-604c1ba9a7ab.

[c] Project ECHO. ECHO Global Health Initiatives in HIV, TB and Health Security. https://hsc.unm.edu/echo/echos-impact/global.html

Source: Author, based on footnote c and AKDN. Improving Health Outcomes in Underserved, Marginalised Regions. http://akdnehrc.org/ehealth_programme/.

Improving Access to Medicines and Technology

119.   Access to medicines for NCDs is a major challenge for countries with high out-of-pocket spending. The cost of NCD medicines is a significant portion of government expenditure on health in the CAREC region. As NCDs become more prevalent, their costs will further strain state budgets. Regional solutions can help address both the cost and quality of medicines for NCDs through increasing domestic pharmaceutical production, and pooled procurement, among others. Access to medicines and vaccines is equally important for combatting CDs.

120.   Strengthening domestic pharmaceutical production, aided by technological transfers, could be a CAREC initiative to address both medicine access and pricing. This may be particularly relevant for CAREC countries that have growing and dynamic pharmaceutical industries, such as Kazakhstan and the Kyrgyz Republic, which are members of a single pharmaceutical market under the EAEU (2015), and Pakistan, which has a growing demand for pharmaceutical production. Multilateral development partners have contributed to the local pharmaceutical production and technology transfer in the region. The WHO, and the International Finance Corporation (IFC) of the World Bank Group, provide direct support for local production, while the Interagency Pharmaceutical Coordination Group facilitates coordination. Under the CAREC framework, ADB and other development partners, as well as CAREC countries (e.g., the PRC), could support

the development of national pharmaceutical industries by facilitating knowledge and technology transfers, and through financing. The CAREC region has the potential of developing into a pharmaceutical export market. Given the single pharmaceutical market creation under EAEU, the point of entry could be through ABEC as Kazakhstan and the Kyrgyz Republic are members of the EAEU (Box 13).

121.   The procurement of medicines is an important component of the medicines supply system, and therefore a major determinant in access to quality medicines. CAREC countries can maximize their limited budgets for medicines through aggregating demand and pooling procurement of medicines, to ensure sustainable supply of quality medicines/vaccines, greater demand predictability, reduced prices, and increased access to medicines.

122.   Pooled procurement is defined as "purchasing done by one procurement office on behalf of a group of facilities, health systems or countries. Group members agree to purchase certain drugs exclusively through the group."[83] Pooled procurement can be established in two ways—through a collaboration agreement (e.g., the Baltic Partnership Agreement[84]) or by establishing a group purchasing organization such as the Pan American Health Organization revolving fund.[85] Public procurement for

---

Box 13: Status of the Common Pharmaceutical Market under Eurasian Economic Union

In 2015, after the Kyrgyz Republic's accession, the Eurasian Economic Union (EAEU) planned to further integrate the pharmaceutical markets to its members. Technical specifications for registration were made stricter and harmonized regulations for the registration of pharmaceuticals were developed. To comply with EAEU rules, amendments in the Kyrgyz Republic law were made. However, due to regulatory complexities associated with unifying the procedures governing pharmaceutical operations through the entire EAEU, the corresponding decision has been delayed,[a] and the fundamental move to the true common market has been postponed to 2025. A transition period until 2025 is foreseen, after which, two registration schemes should be available and producers can decide which scheme they wanted to apply. The centralized scheme works on a mutual recognition base, meaning that registration in one country leads simultaneously to registration in all EAEU countries. If a producer decides to distribute pharmaceuticals only within the Kyrgyz Republic market, national rules will be followed.[b] Although the Kyrgyz Republic system of registration of medical devices is well regarded by other EAEU members, the lack of a qualified pharmaceutical laboratory may be a barrier for the Kyrgyz Republic to fully participate in the EAEU when it comes to regulation of medicines in a fully integrated market.

[a]   E. Vinokurov. 2017. Eurasian Economic Union: Current State and Preliminary Results. *Russian Journal of Economics*. 3 (1). pp. 54–70.
[b]   WHO. 2016. *Pharmaceutical Pricing and Reimbursement Reform in Kyrgyz Republic*. Copenhagen: WHO Regional Office for Europe.
Source: Author based on information from the *Eurasian Economic Commission*. 2017. In the EAEU, a Common Medicines Market Is Launched. 5 May. http://www.eurasiancommission.org/en/nae/news/Pages/5-05-2017.aspx.

---

[83]   WHO. 2007. Multi-country Regional Pooled Procurement of Medicines: Identifying Key Principles for Enabling Regional Pooled Procurement and a Framework for Inter-Regional Collaboration in the African, Caribbean and Pacific Island Countries. Meeting Report. 15-16 January. p. 9. Geneva. https://www.who.int/medicines/publications/PooledProcurement.pdf .

[84]   On 2 May 2012, the three Baltic countries entered into the Baltic Partnership Agreement to carry out joint tenders for purchasing medications and medical equipment as well as lending medications and medical equipment. LIKUMI. 2012. Partnership Agreement between the Ministry of Health of the Republic of Latvia, the Ministry of Social Affairs of the Republic of Estonia, and the Ministry of Health of the Republic of Lithuania on Joint Procurements of Medicinal Products and Medical Devices and Lending of Medicinal Products and Medical Devices Procurable Centrally. https://likumi.lv/doc.php?id=248008.

[85]   PAHO Revolving Fund. https://www.paho.org/hq/index.php?option=com_content&view=article&id=1864:paho-revolving-fund&Itemid=4135&lang=en.

health takes different forms and the best way is through "several public buyers collaborating and potentially pooling resources to negotiate or to buy medical goods and supplies at more favorable conditions."[86] The types of collaboration depend on the level of intensity and range from sharing information on prices and suppliers, to establishing joint procurement through either centralized or decentralized mechanisms. This is a natural progression in collaboration for countries that may want to adopt a less intense type of collaboration at the beginning and move to a more intense approach in the future as procurement systems become more harmonized.[87]

123.   All CAREC countries have been exposed to and participated in pooled procurement initiatives supported by the Global Fund. Of the 11 CAREC countries, 10 have participated in GAVI-supported pooled procurement (Kazakhstan was the exception).[88] A range of regional initiatives can be undertaken to jointly procure medicines, ranging from less intense level (e.g., BeNeLuxA[89]) to more advanced and integrated level (e.g., EU Joint Procurement Agreement) (Box 14). Apart from economies of scale benefits, pooled procurement agreements have also been successfully set up in response to regional health threats.[90]

Box 14: European Union Joint Procurement Agreement

The European Union (EU) Joint Procurement Agreement (JPA) was initiated as a response to the H1N1 pandemic influenza outbreak in 2009, which highlighted the weaknesses in the access and purchasing power of EU countries to obtain pandemic vaccines and medications. The EU-JPA aims to secure more equitable access to specific medical countermeasures and an improved security of supply, with more balanced prices for the participating EU countries. During this public health emergency, countries were competing to acquire scarce supplies, and prices went up as a result. To reduce the chances of similar events occurring in the future, the JPA was signed, to maintain access to vaccines, medicines, and medical equipment that address serious cross-border threats. Provisions for the joint procurement of medical countermeasures are included in Article 5 of Decision 1082/2013/EU on serious cross-border threats to health. As of June 2019, a total of 25 EU countries have signed the JPA.

Source: European Commission. https://ec.europa.eu/health/preparedness_response/overview_en.

---

[86]   J. Espin et al. 2017. How Can Voluntary Cross-Border Collaboration in Public Procurement Improve Access to Health Technologies in Europe? *Policy Brief* 21. Copenhagen: WHO.

[87]   WHO. Procurement Mechanisms and Systems. https://www.who.int/immunization/programmes_systems/procurement/mechanisms_systems/pooled_procurement/en/index1.html.

[88]   The Global Fund transition list includes Azerbaijan, Georgia, Kazakhstan, Pakistan (malaria component), and Turkmenistan. The Global Fund. 2018. *Projected Transitions From Global Fund Support by 2025—Projections by Component.* 15 March. https://www.theglobalfund.org/media/5641/core_projectedtransitionsby2025_list_en.pdf.

[89]   The EU's BeNeLuxA is a group of countries (Austria, Belgium, Luxembourg, and the Netherlands) that have started to collaborate more closely across several fields of health to ensure access to innovative drugs at affordable prices (initially for orphan drugs) through enhancing the patient pool for pharmaceutical companies. BeNeLuxA. https://beneluxa.org/collaboration.

[90]   N. Azzopardi-Muscat, P. Schroder-Back, and H. Brand. 2016. The European Union Joint Procurement Agreement for Cross-Border Health Threats: What is the Potential for this New Mechanism of Health System Collaboration? *Health Economics, Policy and Law.* 12 (1). pp. 43–59. https://www.cambridge.org/core/journals/health-economics-policy-and-law/article/abs/european-union-joint-procurement-agreement-for-crossborder-health-threats-what-is-the-potential-for-this-new-mechanism-of-health-system-collaboration/B1321B80CA68FDFC296FD7DE870746D6.

124.   Accessing and evaluating new technologies is critical in tackling NCDs. Several countries in the region (e.g., Kazakhstan, PRC) have introduced Health Technology Assessments (HTA)[91] and established HTA units to institute new effective and cost-saving technologies into their health systems—basing their purchasing and reimbursement decisions on the results of HTAs. For example, Kazakhstan has implemented HTA in hospital-based settings. The PRC has established a national health development and research center (Box 15) that can be developed into a potential CAREC initiative serving all CAREC countries.

Improving Access to Health Services for Migrants, Mobile Populations, and Border Communities

Access to Health Care for Migrants and Mobile Populations

125.   The economic rationale for providing access to health care for migrant labor is that it saves costs for health care systems of both origin and host countries. Infectious diseases cross borders and often bring associated threat to

---

Box 15: Regional Health Technology Assessment Center in the PRC

The China National Health Development Research Center (CNHDRC) is a government-led health research body established in 2008 to promote, develop, implement, and monitor Health Technology Assessments (HTAs). The People's Republic of China (PRC) HTA network comprises 34 universities, hospitals and providers, research centers, and industry associations and societies, and was launched to incorporate industry expertise in developing methodologies for HTA. In 2010, the CNHDRC collaborated with the United Kingdom's National Institute for Health and Care Excellence (NICE) to combine their extensive experience to promote the institutionalization of HTA among their members. The PRC is also part of a multilateral initiative called HTAsiaLink, which includes Japan; Malaysia; the Philippines; the Republic of Korea; Singapore; Taipei,China; and Thailand. The PRC focuses on capacity building, multistakeholder engagement, information technology infrastructure reforms, and payment reform in pilot hospitals. A set of national HTA guidelines was also developed. In 2018, the National Center for Drug and Technology Assessment was established under CNHDRC to effectively prioritize evidence-based decision-making and optimize resource utilization. The PRC's HTA research results can serve not only the needs of its 33 provinces but also its Central Asia Regional Economic Cooperation (CAREC) Program neighbors. Under its collaboration with NICE, the PRC is establishing a regional center aiming to support neighboring countries with access to new technologies and processes, which are currently inaccessible to many due to budget constraints and long lead-times. However, due to budget constraints and other reasons, HTA is not established in every country. This could be a regional initiative with a lot of potential for cost saving and improving access to new technologies in the CAREC region.

Source: Author based on F. Ruiz and E. Krajenbrink. 2018. Launch of New Chinese Health Ministry Should Help Develop UK—China Partnership in Health Technology Assessment. International Decision Support Initiative (IDSI). https://idsihealth.org/blog/launch-of-new-chinese-health-ministry-should-help-develop-uk-china-partnership-in-health-technology-assessment/; WHO. Healthy China. https://www.who.int/healthpromotion/conferences/9gchp/healthy-china/en/.

---

[91]   As defined by the International Network of Agencies for Health Technology Assessment (INAHTA). HTA studies the medical, social, ethical, and economic implications of development, diffusion, and use of health technology.

migration and livelihoods of migrants and border communities. Improved management of labor migrant flows coupled with ensuring access to health and social protection does not only help mitigate the threat but also increases control of infectious diseases. Hence, migrant labor's access to health care is best addressed through cooperation. Acknowledging this regional issue, CAREC countries have been undertaking efforts at country and regional levels to provide social protection and health care access for migrants, including cooperation in tackling TB in Kazakhstan, the Kyrgyz Republic, and Tajikistan (Box 16).[92]

126.   Central Asian countries (Kazakhstan, the Kyrgyz Republic, Tajikistan, Turkmenistan) have recognized the challenge to "address the root causes of irregular migration," to "reintegrate returning migrant workers," and

help prevent irregular migration by "creating legal migration opportunities." They also made progress in addressing irregular and mixed migration issues at the regional level, particularly within the context of the "Almaty Regional Consultation Process" supported by International Organization for Migration (IOM) and the United Nations High Commissioner for Refugees. The Government of the Kyrgyz Republic and the Government of Tajikistan have promulgated national migration strategies, redesigned national institutional frameworks, established centers to prepare migrants for working abroad, and stepped up outreach efforts to diaspora communities and government counterparts in the Russian Federation. Kazakhstan has included national migrants under its national insurance scheme, which will enter into force in 2020; however, undocumented migrants remain outside of coverage.

Box 16: Cross-Border Cooperation in Migrant Health Care in CAREC

Kazakhstan, the Kyrgyz Republic, and Tajikistan signed bilateral agreements on cross-border cooperation for TB- and MDR-TB control, prevention, and care among migrant workers from Central Asia, and the establishment of a mechanism for exchanging information on TB patients among countries through the Euro WHO TB electronic platform (tbconsilium.org). These agreements were approved as a result of a 3-year program initiated in Kazakhstan in late 2014 with support from the Global Fund to Fight AIDS, Tuberculosis, and Malaria; Project HOPE; the WHO; International Organization for Migration; the Joint United Nations Programme on HIV/AIDS; and the International Federation of Red Cross and Red Crescent Societies. The program is aligned with WHO recommendations for cross-border TB control in Europe and Kazakhstan's national plan to combat TB. A potential entry point for further regional cooperation and integration in this area under CAREC is to deepen the regional dialogue and expand these agreements to engage more countries.

CAREC = Central Asia Regional Economic Cooperation, GAVI = Gavi, the Vaccine Alliance, MDR-TB = multidrug-resistant tuberculosis, TB = tuberculosis, WHO = World Health Organization.
Source. Author based on information provided by WHO; the Global Fund to Fight AIDS, Tuberculosis, and Malaria; GAVI; and Project HOPE partners in stakeholder consultations conducted by author.

---

[92]   The national policy in the PRC aims to ensure that migrants who are registered in their home province can access health care benefits when they migrate to different areas. The IOM states that "Although regular immigrants and stateless persons in the territory of the Republic of Kazakhstan have the right to free medical assistance (GAFMA), irregular and undocumented migrants do not have access to the health care system beyond emergency treatment. In accordance with the Code of the Republic of Kazakhstan, *On People's Health and the Healthcare System*, regular immigrants and stateless persons in the territory of the Republic of Kazakhstan have the right to receive free medical assistance (GAFMA) in the case of acute diseases listed by the Government, unless otherwise stipulated in international agreements. Medical services not included in the GAFMA list are provided when paid for privately." IOM. 2018. Migration Governance Profile: Republic of Kazakhstan. May.

127.   Access to health care by undocumented migrants (with no contracts and health care not covered by the employer) remains to be a significant problem in CAREC. Providing health care for documented migrants remains difficult and its implementation has been slow. One reason is that access to health care is not properly measured. Most countries in the region have a plethora of migration statistical sources (Ministry of Information/Statistics) and administrative data sources. These sources vary across countries, with migration data collected through censuses, sample surveys, and current statistics on migration flows. Statistics offices in some countries collect aggregated reports with migration-related variables from government agencies, such as the Ministry of Interior, the Ministry of Justice (civil registry offices), the Ministry of Education and Science, and the Ministry of Health. Electronic cards for migrants within the region could potentially alleviate the existing data challenges, depending on how these are initiated, and how the data are collected and analyzed. The electronic card for migrants in the Commonwealth of Independent States (CIS) is a good example for CAREC (Box 17).

128.   CAREC can provide technical expertise and knowledge to its member countries to improve migrants' health care in the region through (i) expanding existing bilateral agreements on TB/HIV to include additional services and (ii) supporting the introduction of a series of bilateral agreements that are harmonized with other existing agreements and blocks (e.g., EAEU, CIS) to regulate access to health care for migrant labor. The ADB-supported project for migrant health protection in the GMS under the GMS Health Security Project is a good example for CAREC to consider. The project aims to improve migrant health and mobile populations in areas

---

Box 17: Electronic Cards for Migrants in the Commonwealth Independent States

The Commonwealth of Independent States (CIS)[93] countries are introducing electronic cards for migrant workers under the agreement signed July 2014. These cards contain migrants' personal data such as residence, employment status, health insurance coverage, and educational records. Once the mechanism is introduced, the countries can use the cards to facilitate access to health care for migrants by integrating the cards within an information system to access health services. A referral system between involved countries that ensures migrants receive follow-up services and continue to receive medical aid when needed upon return to their countries of origin would further improve health outcomes and support the prevention and control of outbreaks within the region. So far, five CAREC countries are members of CIS, and the electronic card system can be introduced in the entire CAREC region to benefit its large group of migrant workers with improved health care.

Source: Author based on Government of Belarus, Ministry of Labor and Social Protection. Cooperation within the Commonwealth of Independent States (CIS). http://www.mintrud.gov.by/ru/sng; and Labor Resource Center, St. Petersburg State Autonomous Institution. 2020. Roundtable: Digitalization of the Migration Processes. Ensuring Transparency of Financial Flows in Labor Migration. 28 February. https://gauctr.ru/portfolio/28-fevralya-2020-na-forume-truda-eksperty-obsudili-voprosy-tsifrovizatsii-migratsionnyh-protsessov/.

---

[93]   CAREC members of the CIS include Azerbaijan, Kazakhstan, the Kyrgyz Republic, Tajikistan, and Uzbekistan. Non-CAREC members are Armenia, Belarus, Moldova, and the Russian Federation.

where communicable disease is associated with poverty, poor sanitation, and weak health services.[94]

Access to Health Care for Border Communities

129.   Cooperation in providing health care services across borders is motivated by similar concerns among CAREC countries. Such cooperation aims to bridge the gaps in regional health care provision (due to economic, geographical or health system conditions), and eventually lower the cost of service provision across borders. Services in border areas need to cover various health care services including maternal and child health.[95] Additionally, technology such as telemedicine can facilitate service provision in remote border areas.

130.   A prominent example in the CAREC region is the facility building and service improvement project along the China–Pakistan Economic Corridor (CPEC)—the China Pakistan Fraternity Emergency Care Centre, which was inaugurated in the port city of Gwadar, Pakistan in July 2017.[96] It is the first facility (out of seven planned ones) under the China–Pakistan Life Rescue Corridor running along the CPEC from Gwadar to Kashgar, a PRC border city in Xinjiang Uygur Autonomous Region more than 2,000 kilometers away. Each center is planned to be established according to the model of a community hospital in the PRC, with medical personnel, medical and communication equipment, and an ambulance. It was built to provide medical services to the PRC workers along the CPEC. Prior to 2018, the ratio of patients from the PRC to patients from Pakistan was 8:2, it has since reversed to 2:8. As of 2020 the center was serving a population of 70,000 to 80,000, with the number of patients varying depending on the security situation. In the first 2 weeks of March 2019, it has treated about 290 cases.[97]

131.   There is potential for extending this type of cooperation by aligning and updating building codes and standards in accordance with recommended best practices and regional requirements. This may be especially relevant for the Central Asian countries as well as for Mongolia and the PRC. One additional area for cooperation is building more sustainable, "green" and energy-efficient hospital infrastructure. The health care industry is one of the most energy-consuming and polluting industries. Addressing this challenge by adopting new and improved building codes with guidance on sustainability and energy efficiency would help the region mitigate environmental risks and air pollution (one of the identified risk factors for NCDs).

---

[94]   The GMS region comprises Cambodia, the Lao People's Democratic Republic, Myanmar, the PRC (Yunnan Province and Guangxi Zhuang Autonomous Region), Thailand, and Viet Nam. The GMS has a highly dynamic and complex pattern of fluctuating migration.

[95]   This is also reflected in the CAREC Gender Strategy 2030.

[96]   F. Shabbir. 2019. China–Pakistan Fraternity Emergency Care Center Gwadar Receives 2,302 Patients By December Last . *UrduPoint*. 25 January. https://www.urdupoint.com/en/pakistan/china-pakistan-fraternity-emergency-care-cent-539475.html.

[97]   J. Ma. 2019. The Chinese Medical Clinic in Pakistan on the Belt and Road Security Front Line. *South China Morning Post*. 7 August. https://www.scmp.com/news/china/diplomacy/article/3021650/health-and-safety-chinese-medical-clinic-pakistan-belt-and.

4

CONCLUSIONS FOR CAREC COOPERATION IN HEALTH

4.1 Conclusions

132. **Health as a regional priority.** The increasing threat of newly emerging communicable diseases has been well established for a century, and brought to everyone's doorstep with the current COVID-19 pandemic. Health, social, and economic consequences have been mitigated at high cost. Risk factors such as comorbidity and access to services are better understood. Enabling factors such as population growth, commercial farming, and connectivity are being analyzed and discussed by world leaders. The challenges are to contain COVID-19 and mitigate its socioeconomic impact; to strengthen RHS and health systems and restore growth and stability; and to make development more inclusive and sustainable.

133. **Policy framework.** CAREC countries are signatories to several global commitments and agreements, that provide a common global health policy framework (Chapter 3.1). The WHO's IHR for the control of emerging diseases and other public health events of international importance provide the overall global standards for RHS and are being rolled out at national, regional, national, and local levels. The WHO provides a set of health system standards to move toward UHC and other health-related SDGs, based on the concepts such as PHC and the six WHO building blocks to develop national health systems. The current NCD epidemic that aggravates the COVID-19 impact has triggered stronger commitment to intersector and community-based approaches to promote health and prevent diseases toward health for all by all.

134. **Committed countries.** CAREC countries are committed to eradicate poverty and achieve all SDGs through equitable growth and rural development. In the health sector, CAREC countries strongly support WHO policies and strategies for RHS, PHC, and strengthening national health systems. Most CAREC countries have national health policies and plans that support RHC, and most CAREC countries are in a position to allocate substantial resources to implement these plans. Yet there are often funding gaps due to fiscal constraints and high spending on other national priorities. Similarly, there are also human resource and management challenges that need to be addressed to support health cooperation.

135. **Existing initiatives.** Several agencies and networks are engaged in strengthening RHC, health systems, and cross-border services in CAREC countries such as the GHSA and the One Health initiative (Appendix 5). In view of the COVID-19 pandemic, the Shanghai Cooperation Organization (SCO) has decided to establish a coordination council to jointly counteract disease outbreaks in the SCO space and adopt a plan at the next SCO summit. There are other ongoing bilateral and multilateral initiatives among CAREC countries that can be built on.

136. **Priorities and challenges.** While CAREC countries have a strong case for RHC, regional cooperation has to be relevant and beneficial to all participating countries. RHC and cross-border initiatives should bring clear value addition compared to national solutions. Regional cooperation requires substantial trust and commitment among participating countries in terms of allocation of staff time and funds, political support and leadership for regional health and health diplomacy. RHC further requires clear mandates, responsibilities and interministerial arrangements for regional health, and national plans and strategies that support RHC. Further consultations, assessment and programming will be required to identify the most pressing regional priorities and the feasibility of addressing these through RHC step-by-step.

137. **Regional platform.** Addressing current and future regional health challenges would greatly benefit from the establishment of a joint regional platform for the health sector in CAREC countries. Infectious diseases cross borders and have large externalities. The COVID-19 pandemic will have long-term impact, not only the health sector but on poverty and other risk factors. This will require the mobilization of political support, reforms and resources to deal with the new health agenda. While CAREC countries have many similarities and links, there is currently no overall regional health coordination network for CAREC countries.

138. **CAREC added value.** CAREC is a well-established regional platform with a high-level coordination mechanism, multisector expertise, and experience in mobilization of resources. CAREC and its member countries can build on engagement in health topics such as food hygiene and fortification, SPS, animal health and TADs. Since its inception, the program has been a proactive facilitator of practical, results-based regional projects, and policy initiatives in sectors such as energy and trade in the region. It can serve as a platform to develop regional projects and leverage regional financing. ADB, a convener of CAREC, has been working in RHS in Southeast Asian countries since 2005; and has worked closely with the WHO and other United Nations agencies and other key partners in the health sector. CAREC is well positioned to further strengthen the dialogue and cooperation, support the alignment of different partners, and invest in RHC.

139. **Regional health cooperation development.** In CAREC 2030, the program has broadened its mandate and is in a strong position to support its member countries in RHC. Regional health challenges such as cross-border communicable diseases control, control of NCDs, and health care for migrants and border communities are proposed to be prioritized by its member countries and formulated as a CAREC health strategy toward 2030. This will entail further consultation of stakeholders, assessments, and documentation of ongoing cooperation including with partners. The GMS Health Cooperation Strategy already provides such an example of regional health priorities of the six GMS member countries. Such a strategy would guide programming to facilitate policy dialogue and coordination, information exchange, knowledge sharing and cross learning, and resource mobilization.

4.2 Recommendations

140. Based on the analysis in the preceding chapters, the following recommendations are proposed and for further consideration in the CAREC health strategy. These recommendations are summarized in Table 7.

4.2.1 Strengthening Regional Health Security

141. The ongoing COVID-19 pandemic is a reminder that viruses do not halt at national borders. Countries need to jointly tackle regional health threats. Strengthening RHS requires CAREC cooperation in addressing public health threats from communicable diseases— outbreaks, epidemics, and pandemics such as COVID-19—and in better preparing countries for future public health threats. Several areas for cooperation in RHS can be explored.

142. One key area is regional surveillance, with additional regional modeling and forecasting. Regional surveillance initiatives may include (i) investing in early warning, surveillance, and rapid response systems through improving existing national infrastructure and

regional cooperation on human and animal health surveillance, and their interface, as well as intersector collaboration on human, animal, and plant health; (ii) strengthening laboratory and diagnostic capacity, standards, and quality control through upgrading laboratory facilities, and aligning with regional and international standards; (iii) expanding existing bilateral and multilateral health cooperation initiatives and agreements to involve more CAREC countries; and (iv) enhancing exchange of information and experiences among CAREC countries on cross-border EIDs and TADs, and with countries outside the CAREC region.

143. Strengthening the One Health approach is important toward achieving better public health outcomes. Regional programs, policies, legislation, and research should be in place wherein multiple sectors can communicate and work together. Areas in which the One Health approach is particularly relevant include food safety, the control of zoonoses, and combatting antibiotic resistance.

144. A gradual approach can be considered given the status of cooperation in various areas of surveillance and the significant variations across CAREC in laboratory and diagnostic standards and quality control mechanisms for CDs (animal and human) and NCDs. CAREC countries may further expand sharing information in selected sectors (e.g., human health), and gradually advance the cooperation to establish a regional laboratory network with a reference laboratory to enhance regional laboratory and surveillance capacities. Cooperation activities in regional health surveillance may be implemented through technical assistance projects to review existing capacity at national level and determine the setup of the regional system. Follow-up actions could be linked to country-level laboratory strengthening activities. Many countries are receiving support in response to COVID-19 and are upgrading their health security capabilities such as surveillance. Leveraging regional cooperation under CAREC would add a valuable dimension to ongoing COVID-19 response efforts to build resilient health systems and enhance health security capabilities.

145. In the short term, the focus of RHS cooperation in CAREC can be on containing the COVID-19 pandemic and mitigating its impact on human life and health. These may involve COVID-19-related information sharing, distilling lessons learned and exchange of experiences in disease control, and financing for medical equipment to treat COVID-19 patients and for public protection. A pandemic risk modeling can be developed to help understand the dynamics and mechanisms of COVID-19 and its impact on the region, and to better control and manage the pandemic. CAREC also needs to conduct further in-depth assessments to scope selected regional mechanisms, as well as joint capacity building and simulation exercises that can strengthen RHS based on lessons from the COVID-19 pandemic.

Strengthening Health Systems Through Regional Cooperation

146. Responsive health systems within CAREC countries provide foundations for ensuring RHC. Cooperation can focus on building health systems capacities in addressing national and regional health threats. This may include preparing for and managing future global and regional health threats such as COVID-19, and preventing and managing NCDs.

147. **Human resources for health.** Increasing the comparability and mutual recognition of educational qualifications in health profession allows more mobility for health students and professionals within CAREC. A first step could be assessing health workforce requirements to support national health strategies toward achieving universal health coverage and SDGs, as well as the potential for regional collaboration. Future initiatives may include creating migrant

health worker databases linked with employer databases (hospitals and clinics), and facilitating information exchange for both migrants and employers. Other areas for cooperation could be improving the capacity to predict and respond to health "market" needs (both public and private), and training for skills improvement. Officially capturing and sharing migrant health worker demographic, occupational, and health data can help match health professionals' skills supply and demand. The proper matching of labor supply and demand can support countries in increasing revenue from remittances—since health professionals would be hired in accordance with their skills—and eventually enhance skills and capacity in origin countries as the workers return. An important factor to consider is that the Russian Federation, which is not a CAREC member country, is the biggest "pull" for migrants in the region. This factor should be taken into consideration when devising joint initiatives for migrant health workers in the CAREC region.

148.   **Health information systems.**
Regional cooperation on improving health information systems can focus on (i) advancing interoperability of fragmented health information system at national level facilitated by national eHealth strategies, (ii) facilitating harmonization of eHealth standards and strategy at regional level, and (iii) exploring how innovative ICT can strengthen RHC. This can be achieved through further investment in ICT technologies, such as eHealth and telemedicine, to (i) improve access to training, data collection and analysis, and diagnostic and clinical decision-making support; and (ii) link underserved communities (including cross-border communities) to health

care institutions and providers to provide access to low-cost, equitable health services, and help minimize the barriers of distance and time. Further, the WHO's One Health approach adopted by Afghanistan, Azerbaijan, Kazakhstan, and Pakistan,[98] and the EIDSS adopted in Georgia and Kazakhstan can be expanded to improve the management of human, animal, and environmental health in the region. The first step could be to invest in creating and sharing knowledge (health information, data, and experience) among interested countries on a pilot basis, which can be expanded later across the whole region.

149.   **Access to medicines and technology.**
CAREC countries can work together to improve access to medicines and technologies and achieve lowered cost and improved quality of medicines. These can be done by (i) facilitating pharmaceutical manufacturing in the region through transfer of technologies, and (ii) pooling of procurement of medicines in the region for economies of scale. Given the different regulatory policies and weak capacities to harmonize regulatory systems across the region, information sharing, reliance policies, and HTA can be a starting point, which can be gradually deepened into joint procurement of medicines and quality control. CAREC could provide a framework for regional dialogue between interested parties and explore reliance policies and regulatory coordination (e.g., for COVID-19 vaccines). There is also significant potential for developing a single pharmaceutical market in the CAREC region through joint ventures such as combining domestic pharmaceutical productions, with a significant role for the private sector.

---

[98]   One Health is an approach advocated by the WHO "to designing and implementing programs, policies, legislation, and research in which multiple sectors communicate and work together to achieve better public health outcomes." WHO. One Health. https://www.who.int/news-room/q-a-detail/one-health.

Improving Access to Health Services for Migrants, Mobile Populations, and Border Communities

150.   Multiple modalities for regional cooperation in improving health services exist, ranging from (i) improving data collection and sharing information on access to health care for migrants, (ii) improving information at pre-departure stages, (iii) updating and harmonizing provisions for access under bilateral agreements, and (iv) introducing fully pledged migrant health insurance schemes. Several CAREC countries are part of existing agreements under the CIS and EAEU framework. Activities are ongoing to move toward broader health insurance coverage for migrant workers. Regional insurance schemes are complex and require a deeper level of integration for successful implementation. CAREC cooperation in this

area may require a series of investment projects involving subgroups of countries with a strong common goal of improving access to health care for migrants. This could involve deepening the scope of current agreements, expanding them to additional countries, or facilitating the implementation of existing agreements by supporting countries bound by bilateral or multilateral agreements.

151.   There is potential to further assess cross-border health services along the CAREC economic corridors and further scope feasibility of cross-border specialty care. Work has been undertaken to upgrade cross-border facilities and enhance infrastructure and capacity, including for migrant workers. Joint regional strategies could support protecting the most vulnerable residing in border areas (women, the elderly, children, persons with disabilities, and migrant and mobile populations) from disease outbreaks and improve their access to health services.

4.3 Proposed Institutional Arrangements and Next Steps

152.   Health is a new sector under the CAREC Program; and health cooperation will help address health risks and ensure RHC. Advancing regional cooperation requires a regional health strategy and an institutional setup with clarified scope and responsibilities among stakeholders. Taking into consideration health cooperation in other regions and/or subregions (e.g., the GMS), a working group composed of sector officials and health experts in CAREC countries can be established as a first step, to provide guidance in formulating a CAREC regional health strategy following the completion of this scoping study and to discuss options for institutionalizing regional cooperation for health under CAREC.

153.   Given the region's close economic and social ties with neighbors that are not part of

CAREC—especially with some important regional players (e.g., India, Iran, the Russian Federation)—CAREC should also strengthen collaboration with other regional cooperation mechanisms including the Economic Cooperation Organization, the Shanghai Cooperation Organization, the South Asian Association for Regional Cooperation, Organization for Islamic Cooperation and several others (Appendix 5 Table A5.1). This is to jointly address public health risks and global health threats like COVID-19, and consider cooperation modalities under the emerging CAREC health framework.

154.   Based on the analysis of priority needs and potential areas for regional cooperation, it is recommended that CAREC members

commence discussions on health cooperation and formulate an RHC strategy toward 2030, outlining common goals, shared health challenges, and priorities for cooperation, with possibly three objectives:

- Strengthen RHS through a series of regional efforts. These include enhancing regional rapid response, surveillance, and recovery efforts through infrastructure and human resource strengthening, increasing information sharing and coordination on health data and use of ICT, and improving coordination at the human–animal health nexus.
- Build resilient health systems through regional cooperation for effective control of CDs and NCDs based on WHO building blocks as the solid foundations for RHC.

These include access to quality medicines and services, human resources for health and skills recognition, health information systems and surveillance, information sharing and aggregating demand, and cross-border services.
- Improve health services for migrants, mobile populations, and people living in border communities including improving access to cross-border services, health insurance, and screening and reporting.

155.   These interconnected objectives may support the overarching goal of addressing pandemic risks and control of CDs, prevention and treatments of NCDs under the CAREC 2030 strategy, and improving health care services of the migrant workers in the CAREC region.

Table 8: Summary of Recommendations

Area of Cooperation	Recommendations
Strengthening regional health security	Short-term (up to 3 years) • Assess potential for collaboration in controlling emerging and chronic infectious diseases (completed through this scoping study) • Distill lessons learned from COVID-19 pandemic and response to further strengthen regional health security • Continue strengthening national health security capabilities such as surveillance systems to support regional health cooperation • Assess potential for establishment of regional laboratory capacity for quality control and assurance • Strengthen regional preparedness and response coordination for emerging and chronic infectious diseases control • Scope potential for other regional mechanisms that will strengthen health security such as joint outbreak investigation, regional asset management, and stockpiling for rapid response • Promote knowledge, information, and data sharing on infectious diseases of regional relevance • Strengthen timely sharing of information and surveillance data on infectious diseases, including risk assessment results • Pilot regional approaches based on ongoing projects

continued on next page

Table 8 *continued*

Area of Cooperation	Recommendations
	Medium- to long-term (over the next 3 to 10 years) • Develop joint prevention, surveillance, and response capacity for infectious diseases • Strengthen human-animal health coordination to control zoonosis (One Health approach) • Explore use of innovative ICT in enhancing regional health surveillance and information sharing (disease codification, privacy provisions, data management standards and data sharing) • Strengthen and harmonize regional standards and regulation (e.g., with International Health Regulations) • Improve regional health security infrastructure (laboratory, waste management, surge capacity, rapid response) • Develop sustainable financing mechanisms to prevent and control regional health threats
Supporting health systems development through regional cooperation	Short-term (up to 3 years) • Support development of regional and national eHealth strategies and plans • Assess potential for strengthening regulatory coordination and reliance policies (e.g., COVID-19 vaccines) • Assess health workforce requirements in CAREC countries to support national health strategies and achievement of SDGs by 2030 and potential for regional collaboration • Promote knowledge, information, and data sharing on NCDs and related risk factors Medium- to long-term (over the next 3 to 10 years) • Support harmonization of regulatory provisions in procurement and information sharing for medicines, and regulate the trade and quality control of medicines in the region • Establish mutual recognition of skills of health professionals • Explore opportunities for private sector involvement in promoting access to medicines, improving domestic production capacity, and technology transfer • Assess capacity for further cooperation around high-level medical technology for health
Improving health services for migrants, mobile populations, and border communities	Short-term (up to 2 years) • Strengthen cross-border management of migrant health services • Assess current state of portability of health care benefits and liabilities across borders • Assess potential for health services development along CAREC economic corridors (e.g., Almaty–Bishkek Economic Corridor) • Stock-take specialty care and potential for cross-border services for specialty care • Develop joint strategies to protect the most vulnerable residing in border areas (women, the elderly, children, persons with disabilities, and migrant and mobile populations) from disease outbreaks and improve their access to health services Medium- to long-term (over the next 10 years) • Support regional collaboration in access and financing of health services for migrants • Develop referral services along CAREC economic corridors
Institutional arrangements under CAREC	• Conduct regional dialogue to appraise the interests of governments, partners, and other stakeholders • Establish a CAREC regional coordination mechanism for the health sector. This could begin with (i) constituting a working group composed of senior health sector officials from CAREC member countries with the task to deliberate on the findings and recommendations of this scoping study and (ii) identifying immediate and short-term activities to promote regional health cooperation. • Develop medium- to long-term CAREC regional health cooperation strategy toward 2030 through a participatory planning process • Strengthen collaboration with CAREC's major neighboring countries in addressing regional health threats

CAREC = Central Asia Regional Economic Cooperation, COVID-19 = coronavirus disease, ICT = information and communication technology, SDG = Sustainable Development Goal, NCD = noncommunicable disease.

Source: Author.

APPENDIX 1
SELECTED INDICATORS

Table A1.1: Socioeconomic Indicators

Indicators	AFG	AZE	PRC	GEO	KAZ	KGZ	MON	PAK	TAJ	TKM	UZB
GDP growth (annual %), 2018	1.0	1.4	6.6	4.8	4.1	3.5	7.2	5.8	7.3	6.2	5.1
GDP per capita, current $, 2018	521	4,721	9,771	4,717	9,813	1,281	4,122	1,482	827	6,967	1,532
GNI per capita, Atlas method (current international $), 2018	550	4,050	9,460	4,440	8,070	1,220	3,660	1,590	1,010	6,740	2,020
GDP per capita, PPP, current $, 2018	1,955	18,044	18,237	12,005	27,880	3,885	13,800	5,567	3,450	19,304	8,556
GDP per capita, PPP, constant 2011 international $, 2018	1,735	16,011	16,182	10,652	24,738	3,447	12,245	4,940	3,061	17,129	7,592
Poverty headcount ratio at national poverty line (% of the population), 2018 or as referred	54.5[a]	6.0[b]	1.7	20.1	2.5	22.4	28.4	24.3[c]	27.4	...	14.1[d]
Current health expenditure per capita (current $), 2018	49.8	165.8	501.1	312.8	275.9	85.7	155.1	42.9	59.8	460.2	82.3
Current health expenditure per capita, PPP (current international $), 2018	186.4	633.6	935.2	795.9	783.8	259.9	519.3	178.2	249.8	1,275.2	459.4
Current health expenditure (% of GDP), 2018	9.4	3.5	5.4	7.1	2.9	6.5	3.8	3.2	7.2	6.6	5.3
Out-of-pocket expenditure (% of current health expenditure), 2018	78.4	72.8	35.8	47.7	33.5	52.4	32.4	56.2	68.4	76.3	60.3

... = data not available, AFG = Afghanistan, AZE = Azerbaijan, GDP = gross domestic product, GEO = Georgia, GNI = gross national income, KAZ = Kazakhstan, KGZ = Kyrgyz Republic, MON = Mongolia, PAK = Pakistan, PPP = purchasing power parity, PRC = People's Republic of China, TAJ = Tajikistan, TKM = Turkmenistan, UZB = Uzbekistan.

[a] 2016
[b] 2012
[c] 2015
[d] 2013

Note: Data for Turkmenistan on poverty headcount ratio at national poverty line are not available from the source at the time of publication.

Source: World Bank. World Development Indicators. https://data.worldbank.org/topic/economy-and-growth?view=chart (accessed 21 January 2019, 12 June 2020 and 3 May 2021).

Table A1.2: Demographic Indicators

Indicators	AFG	AZE	PRC	GEO	KAZ	KGZ	MON	PAK	TAJ	TKM	UZB
Population, total (million), 2018	37.2	9.9	1,392.7	3.7	18.3	6.3	3.2	212.2	9.1	5.9	33.0
Population, female (% of total population), 2018	48.6	50.1	48.7	52.3	51.5	50.5	50.7	48.5	49.6	50.8	50.1
Population, male (% of total population), 2018	51.4	49.9	51.3	47.7	48.5	49.5	49.3	51.5	50.4	49.2	49.9
Annual population growth rate (%), 2018	2.4	0.9	0.5	0.0	1.3	2.0	1.8	2.1	2.5	1.6	1.7
Population ages 0–14 (% of total population), 2018	43.1	23.4	17.9	19.8	28.5	32.4	30.4	35.3	36.8	30.8	28.7
Population ages 15–64 (% of total population), 2018	54.3	70.4	71.2	65.3	64.1	63.2	65.5	60.4	60.2	64.8	66.9
Population ages 65 and above (% of total population), 2018	2.6	6.2	10.9	14.9	7.4	4.5	4.1	4.3	3.0	4.4	4.4

AFG = Afghanistan, AZE = Azerbaijan, GEO = Georgia, KAZ = Kazakhstan, KGZ = Kyrgyz Republic, MON = Mongolia, PAK = Pakistan, PRC = People's Republic of China, TAJ = Tajikistan, TKM = Turkmenistan, UZB = Uzbekistan.

Source: World Bank. World Development Indicators. https://datacatalog.worldbank.org/dataset/population-estimates-and-projections (accessed 21 January 2019).

Table A1.3 Selective Health and Health Services Indicators

Indicators	AFG	AZE	PRC	GEO	KAZ	KGZ	MON	PAK	TAJ	TKM	UZB
Life expectancy at birth, female (years), 2017	65.7	75.2	78.8	77.8	76.9	75.4	73.8	67.9	80.5	73.0	73.5
Life expectancy at birth, male (years), 2017	62.7	70.1	74.3	69.0	68.7	67.2	65.5	66.0	68.5	64.5	69.3
Maternal mortality ratio per 100,000 live births), 2017	638.0	26.0	29.0	25.0	10.0	60.0	45.0	140.0	17.0	7.0	29.0
Mortality rate, infant (per 1,000 live births), 2018	47.9	19.2	7.4	8.7	8.8	16.9	14.0	57.2	30.4	39.3	19.1
Mortality rate, under 5 (per 1,000 live births), 2018	62.3	21.5	8.6	9.8	9.9	18.9	16.3	69.3	34.8	45.8	21.4
Mortality rate, neonatal (per 1,000 live births), 2018	37.1	11.2	4.3	5.9	5.6	13.2	8.7	42.0	15.0	21.0	11.6
Cause of death, by communicable diseases and maternal, prenatal and nutrition conditions (% of total), 2016	36.4	8.8	3.8	2.7	4.5	9.6	9.7	34.9	23.2	17.2	10.3
Cause of death, by non-communicable diseases (% of total), 2016	44.1	86.6	89.3	93.7	86.0	82.7	79.7	57.8	69.2	76.2	83.7
Cause of death, by accidents and injuries, 2016	19.5	4.6	6.9	3.6	9.5	7.7	10.6	7.3	7.6	6.6	6.0
Births attended by skilled health staff (% of total), 2018	58.8	99.4	99.9[a]	99.4	99.9	98.8	98.3	69.3	94.8	100.0[a]	100.0
Nurses and midwives (per 1,000 people), 2014	0.3	7.0	2.3[b]	4.1[b]	8.5[c]	6.4[c]	4.0[a]	0.5[b]	5.2	4.6	12.1
Hospital beds (per 1,000 people), 2013	0.5[b]	4.7	4.2[d]	2.6	6.7	4.5	7.0[d]	0.6[e]	4.8	7.4	4.0

GDP = gross domestic product, GNI = gross national income, PPP = purchasing power parity, AFG = Afghanistan, AZE = Azerbaijan, GEO = Georgia, KAZ = Kazakhstan, KGZ = Kyrgyz Republic, MON = Mongolia, PAK = Pakistan, PRC = People's Republic of China, TAJ = Tajikistan, TKM = Turkmenistan, UZB = Uzbekistan.

[a] 2016

[b] 2012

[c] 2015

[d] 2013

Source: World Bank. World Development Indicators. https://data.worldbank.org/topic/economy-and-growth?view=chart (accessed 21 January 2019 and 12 June 2020).

APPENDIX 2
CAREC HEALTH SYSTEMS DEVELOPMENT BASED ON WHO BUILDING BLOCKS

1.   The World Health Organization (WHO) health systems building blocks represent the state of the national health care systems and indicate the performance levels in terms of quality, efficiency, equity, and sustainability (Figure A2.1). These building blocks are all interconnected and form the foundations of the regional health landscape.

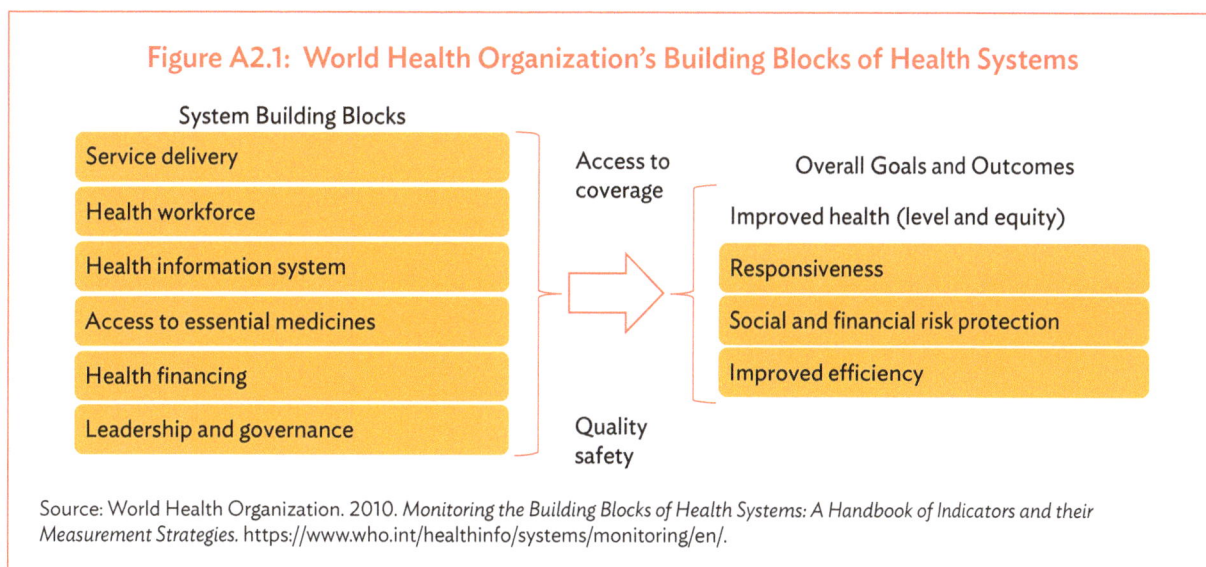

Figure A2.1: World Health Organization's Building Blocks of Health Systems

System Building Blocks

- Service delivery
- Health workforce
- Health information system
- Access to essential medicines
- Health financing
- Leadership and governance

Access to coverage

Quality safety

Overall Goals and Outcomes

Improved health (level and equity)

- Responsiveness
- Social and financial risk protection
- Improved efficiency

Source: World Health Organization. 2010. *Monitoring the Building Blocks of Health Systems: A Handbook of Indicators and their Measurement Strategies.* https://www.who.int/healthinfo/systems/monitoring/en/.

Health Services Delivery

2.   Health service delivery systems are diverse across the Central Asia Regional Economic Cooperation (CAREC) Program region.[1] There are substantial variations in terms of public–private mix, services mix, human resources, and financing. Most of the former Soviet Union republics, following independence, have gone through a rationalization process in terms of hospital and health staff, and have strongly promoted family medicine. These countries have typically retained a two-pillar system

---

[1]   D. Balabanova et al. 2013. Good Health at Low Cost 25 Years On: Lessons for the Future of Health Systems Strengthening. *The Lancet.* 381 (2). pp. 2118–2133.

of clinical and sanitary services. The former Soviet Union republics have inherited an extensive but inefficient health infrastructure, and they are faced with limited revenue. They focus on reducing hospital bed capacity, investing in the development of general practice (family medicine) models, replacing former polyclinics, and changing primary care financing to a capitation-based model.[2] Bed numbers in these countries dropped substantially in the 1990s and now closely resemble the levels seen in other parts of Europe (Figure A2.2). There are also efforts to improve allocative efficiency, with an increasing share of resources devoted to the reformed primary health care (PHC) system, often supported by donor funding. Kazakhstan and Turkmenistan, both generating revenues from oil and gas, have embarked on major new investments in infrastructure in recent years.[3]

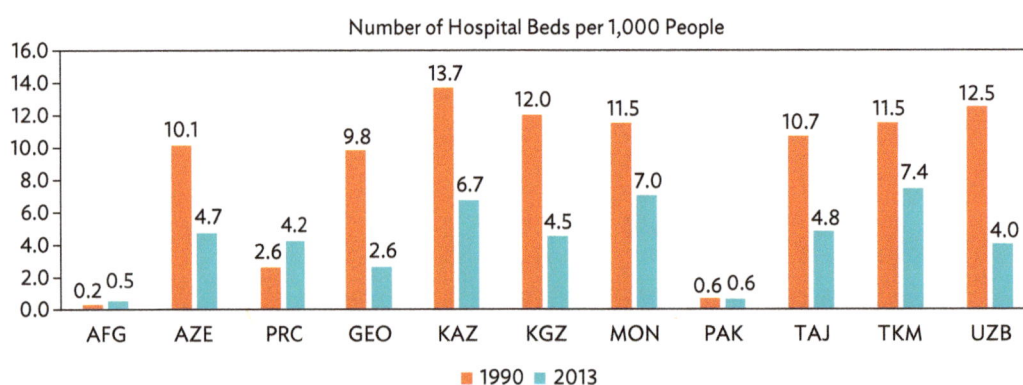

Figure A2.2: Hospital Bed Density in CAREC Countries

Number of Hospital Beds per 1,000 People

■ 1990 ■ 2013

AFG = Afghanistan, AZE = Azerbaijan , CAREC = Central Asia Regional Economic Cooperation, GEO = Georgia, KAZ = Kazakhstan, KGZ = Kyrgyz Republic, MON = Mongolia, PAK = Pakistan, PRC = People's Republic of China, TAJ = Tajikistan, TKM = Turkmenistan, UZB = Uzbekistan.

Source: World Health Organization. Global Health Observatory. https://www.who.int/data/gho (accessed 6 February 2020).

3.   According to the universal health coverage (UHC) index, service coverage for the CAREC region is quite high in most countries (Table A2.1). The UHC index is a composite measure of 16 indicators. The index assesses health services in a population using criteria in four main categories: (i) reproductive, maternal, newborn, and child health (RMNCH); (ii) infectious diseases; (iii) noncommunicable diseases (NCDs); and (iv) service capacity and access. According to this index, among the CAREC countries, only Afghanistan scores poorly, followed by Pakistan. The average for the WHO European Region (which include all CAREC countries except Afghanistan, Mongolia, Pakistan, and the People's Republic of China [PRC]) is at 77. The global average is at 66. Nevertheless, challenges in service delivery remain across the region.

---

2   T. Ensor and R. Thompson. 1999. Rationalizing Rural Hospital Services in Kazakhstan. *The International Journal of Health Planning and Management*. 14 (2). Capitation payment is a regular sum paid per enrolled person assigned to the physician whether or not that person seeks care. The amount of remuneration is based on the average expected health care utilization of that patient, with payment for patients generally varying by age and health status. Providers who work under such plans focus on preventive health care.

3   B. Rechel et al. 2009. *Health in Turkmenistan after Niyazov*. London. London School of Hygiene and Tropical Medicine; and Médecins Sans Frontières. 2010. Turkmenistan's Opaque Health System. Amsterdam. April. https://www.doctorswithoutborders.org/what-we-do/news-stories/research/turkmenistans-opaque-health-system.

Table A2.1: Universal Health Coverage Index for CAREC Countries

Country	UHC Index of Service Coverage (2017)
Afghanistan	37
Azerbaijan	65
China, People's Republic of	79
Georgia	66
Kazakhstan	76
Kyrgyz Republic	70
Mongolia	62
Pakistan	45
Tajikistan	68
Turkmenistan	70
Uzbekistan	73

CAREC = Central Asia Regional Economic Cooperation, UHC = universal health coverage, WHO = World Health Organization.

Source: WHO. Global Health Observatory. http://apps.who.int/gho/data/view.main.INDEXOFESSENTIALSERVICECOVERAGEv (accessed 6 February 2020).

4.   The PRC has made significant strides in increasing access to services, but as its population gets richer and older, the health care system is under strain to ensure the delivery of services to a growing demand. Urban hospitals often suffer from overcrowding, while rural populations in remote areas still lack access to basic health services. A 2018 study revealed that in Afghanistan, money is the most important barrier to accessing institutional delivery (56%), followed by lack of transportation (37%), and family restrictions (30%).[4] For vulnerable groups, perceived availability of health care and experience with coverage has not improved markedly over the last 10 years (footnote 3).

5.   A significant portion of the CAREC region's population still lacks access to essential health services in rural areas. Where health care is accessible, it is often fragmented and of poor quality. Continuity of care is hampered by poor coordination across providers and a lack of integration with other critical sectors (e.g., social services). The predominance of curative care models based on hospitals, donor-driven vertical programs, and single diseases further compounds the problem, making service provision costly, inefficient, and difficult to manage.

6.   The private health sector has been developing in CAREC countries, especially in PHC but less so in hospital services. For example, in Afghanistan, private health services provide about two-thirds of all health services, including in rural areas. Some countries like Georgia have opted for a private practitioner model, while Pakistan has devolved health services to provincial level and is moving toward public-private partnerships. Domestic private health expenditure (as a percentage of current health expenditure) ranges from 37.8% (Kazakhstan) to 77.6% (Turkmenistan).[5] This has implications not

---

[4]   A. Higgins et al. 2018. Barriers Associated with Care-Seeking for Institutional Delivery among Rural Women in Three Provinces in Afghanistan. *BMC Pregnancy Childbirth*. 18. p. 246. https://doi.org/10.1186/s12884-018-1890-2.

[5]   World Bank. Data. Domestic Private Health Expenditure (% of Current Health Expenditure). https://data.worldbank.org/indicator/SH.XPD.PVTD.CH.ZS (accessed 16 November 2020).

only on the range of health services and their affordability for the poor, but also on surveillance and reporting. Even if regulation of private health services is in place, it is often not enforced.

7.   The organization of health systems has public health implications in terms of the provision of preventive services, equity in access to services, the quality of care, financing, and monitoring. Epidemic response capacity is under federal control, but depends on the support of the provinces and various public and private service providers. In the regional context, PHC is essential in epidemic control, serving as the first level of contact where infections are first identified.

8.   Quality clinical laboratories are essential for improving health care and public health and an important aspect of health service delivery. The WHO is leading efforts to upgrade laboratory services.[6] Most CAREC countries have a large number of operating laboratories, but with low-quality services and unreliable test results. Because the public does not trust the test results, patients seek testing in several laboratories (so-called laboratory shopping). Countries also lack qualified laboratory personnel and many laboratories use outdated equipment. Laboratory equipment is not used properly due to lack of management and maintenance regulations. Most CAREC countries lack an internationally recognized laboratory certification system. With the coronavirus disease (COVID-19), investment in upgrading laboratory services has accelerated. Generally, laboratory services in the CAREC region remain fragmented.[7] There have been overstaffing of the actual workload, duplication of functions, and insufficient access to international laboratory networks. Funding sources and levels for various health services networks in CAREC differ. Clinical laboratories, while mostly government-funded, also seek private financing, or they become exclusively and privately funded. Oversight of privately funded and operated laboratories remains unregulated or poorly regulated, often leading to poor data collection on private sector activities and private facilities not being captured in government databases. This is particularly a problem for countries (e.g., Georgia, Mongolia, Uzbekistan) where much of the service provision is done by the private sector.

Health Workforce

9.   While all former Soviet Republics, at independence, inherited a relatively large health workforce and a large number of physicians per capita, other countries in the region have historically suffered from an acute shortage of health workers due to conflict, upheaval, and geographic isolation. As a result of these differences in historical starting points, the trends in human resources for health (HRH) look completely different in the CAREC subregions. Over the last 3 decades, HRH numbers have decreased significantly in countries of the former Soviet Union; while in Afghanistan, Pakistan, and the PRC, the numbers have been steadily rising.

10.   There are also significant variations in absolute numbers of HRH across the region, with the number of physicians ranging from 30 per 100,000 population in Afghanistan to 510 per 100,000 population in Georgia (one of the highest rates in the WHO European Region) (Table A2.2). The geographic distribution of HRH and personnel specialization and quality are unbalanced in most of the CAREC countries. Health workers tend to concentrate in the capitals or large cities; thus rural and

---

[6]   WHO. 2018. Better Labs for Better Health: Strengthening Laboratory Systems in the WHO European Region. *Report of the Third Partners Meeting with a Focus on Antimicrobial Resistance.* Copenhagen.

[7]   WHO's Mongolia joint external evaluation (JEE) and Kyrgyz Republic JEE have pointed this out.

remote areas experience shortages. Most countries have attempted to attract doctors to rural and remote areas and retain them, for example, by providing higher-quality accommodation, opportunities for career growth and education, and other social benefits such as increased salaries.[8] In terms of specialization, primary care suffers from shortages of personnel, despite the increasing supply of health professionals. Policies in many countries anticipate a shift from hospital to primary care settings. However, in practice, in many countries of the former Soviet Union, the ratio of health workers working in secondary and tertiary care has remained fairly high while the number of general practitioners per capita, albeit growing, remains low. This is also a problem for the PRC as it faces an aging population; the requirements for PHC physicians are growing faster than their supply. There is simultaneously a concern related to health workers moving from the public to the private sector, due to higher wages.[9]

Table A2.2: Density of Health Personnel in CAREC and Other Regions

Country/Region	Nurses and Midwives (per 1,000 people)	Physicians (per 1,000 people)	Surgical Workforce (per 1,000 people)
Afghanistan	0.3	0.3	0.0
Azerbaijan	7.0	3.4	0.7
Georgia	4.1	5.1	1.3
Kazakhstan	8.5	3.3	0.9
Kyrgyz Republic	6.4	1.9	0.5
Mongolia	4.0	2.9	0.5
Pakistan	0.5	1.0	0.1
China, People's Republic of	2.3	1.8	0.4
Tajikistan	5.2	1.7	0.6
Turkmenistan	4.6	2.2	0.6
Uzbekistan	12.1	2.4	0.5
Europe	8.1	3.4	0.8
Low income countries	0.9	0.3	0.0
Lower middle-income countries	1.8	0.7	0.1
Upper middle-income countries	3.5	2.0	0.4
High-income countries	8.8	3.0	0.7

CAREC= Central Asia Regional Economic Cooperation.
Source: World Health Organization. Global Health Observatory. https://www.who.int/data/gho (accessed 6 February 2020).

---

[8] A. Katsaga et al. 2012. *Kazakhstan: Health System Review, Health Systems in Transition.* Vol 14(4). pp. 1-154. https://pubmed.ncbi.nlm.nih.gov/22894852.

[9] F. Ibrahimov et al. 2010. Azerbaijan: Health System Review. *Health Systems in Transition.* 12 (3). pp. 1-115. January; World Health Organization. Regional Office for Europe. European Observatory on Health Systems and Policies. *Copenhagen.* https://apps.who.int/iris/handle/10665/330333.

Health Information Systems

11.   To meet the emerging challenges of an aging population, changing disease patterns, increasingly complex health care needs, and scarce resources, health systems have to fundamentally transform the way they use data. Effective use of digital technology and electronic data can help improve the delivery of health care, strengthen health system governance, ensure that resource allocation is based on needs, and help inform patients so that they can manage actively their own health care. All of these can contribute to improving population health and achieving other policy objectives, such as efficiency gains.

12.   Most health information management systems in the CAREC region are fragmented, with data collection and compilation undertaken by various institutions and programs at provincial or regional level and compiled by a national body. Institutions and programs perform data collection and compilation using different methods, resulting in overlapping data collection systems (digital and paper-based), data gaps, and inconsistencies. This fragmentation makes the collection process cumbersome, and the data analysis difficult and unreliable for evidenced-based decision-making.[10] Separate vertical disease-oriented information systems also contribute to this challenge. Vertical donor-funded programs (tuberculosis [TB], HIV, immunization) in many countries have contributed to establishing the much-needed surveillance. However, donor-driven collection and analysis processes and products have inadvertently contributed to disintegration within national reporting structures.[11] An additional problem of data quality affects most systems, since at the facility level, reporting forms are often numerous and burdensome, due to the existence of multiple data collection systems and the uneven quality of reporting (rarely verified by an independent body). Oftentimes data are not sex-disaggregated making it difficult to retrieve information on women's health status.

Access to Medicines and Technology

13.   Access to available, affordable, and quality medicines in the CAREC region remains challenging.[12] In some countries, such as Pakistan, where public procurement of medicines has been efficient in achieving low prices, supply is inadequate to cover the needs of patients from government health facilities; and medicines, such as in Mongolia and Pakistan, are much less affordable when purchased in the private sector.[13] In countries where availability of medicines is better, even generics tend to be overpriced (Kazakhstan, Mongolia, Tajikistan). In the Kyrgyz Republic, the government only pays for 10% of the cost of medicines, which are the second-largest expenditure for most families after food. High markups contribute to the high costs of medicines in some CAREC countries, which can

---

[10]   WHO. Pakistan Health Information System. http://www.emro.who.int/pak/programmes/health-managment-information-system.html.

[11]   J. S. Ancker et al. 2013. Sociotechnical Challenges to Developing Technologies for Patient Access to Health Information Exchange Data. *Journal of the American Medical Informatics Association.* September. 21 (4).

[12]   Affordability is calculated as the number of days the lowest paid unskilled government worker would have to work to pay for medicines for one month's treatment of chronic conditions, or a course of treatment for acute conditions.

[13]   WHO Health Action International (HAI). 2008. *Pakistan: Medicine Prices, Availability, Affordability and Price Components.* https://haiweb.org/wp-content/uploads/2015/07/Pakistan-Summary-Report-Pricing-Surveys.pdf; and WHO HAI. 2012. *Mongolia: Medicine Prices, Availability, Affordability and Price Components Surveys.* https://haiweb.org/wp-content/uploads/2015/07/Mongolia-Summary-Pricing-Surveys.pdf.

reach 130%.[14] As a result of such variability, several CAREC countries (Azerbaijan, Kazakhstan, the Kyrgyz Republic, and Uzbekistan) have adopted laws to regulate pricing. There have been reductions in procurement prices (Kyrgyz Republic), especially for treatment of priority health conditions that are covered under national insurance plans and are included in state guaranteed benefits packages. However, treatment of acute and chronic conditions remains expensive (requiring 5 to 15 daily wages in the Kyrgyz Republic).[15]

14. There are significant regional differences in quality control and laboratory capacity. The PRC has the most advanced and well-established pharmaceutical industry. However, it faces significant quality challenges due to stringent regulation, fragmentation between national and administrative levels lack of bioequivalence testing and strong good manufacturing practice standards, and distribution chain and market fragmentation.[16] The study of Verhoeven (2018) on pharmaceutical quality assurance in the Almaty–Bishkek Economic Corridor (ABEC) indicates that the quality of medicines assurance system in Kazakhstan is reliable and testing criteria are aligned with European standards, and the equipment in the laboratories is modern with adequate human capacity to carry it out.[17] Despite the progress achieved in the region, quality control and laboratory capacity in some countries are still suboptimal, mainly constrained by poor infrastructure even with new legislation implemented (such as in the Kyrgyz Republic in 2017).[18]

15. Pakistan has recently undertaken many reforms to ensure the delivery of safe and efficacious medicines. The country established in 2012 an autonomous Drug Regulatory Authority, and is currently developing and implementing a comprehensive national pharmacovigilance system.[19] In November 2018, Pakistan acquired full membership status to the WHO's Programme for International Drug Monitoring. However, there is still insufficient capacity, mostly hampered by lack of funding for drug testing. In most CAREC countries, quality control of medicines in the public and private sectors is given low priority, often depending on outdated laboratory facilities and field capacity resulting in limited testing and public health measures.

16. Regulation of health products requires significant technical expertise and sustainable funding. With great variation in capacities and resources across CAREC, the proper and timely regulation of new health products can improve access to quality-assured health products in the region. Few CAREC countries regulate medical devices despite their critical roles to prevent, diagnose, and treat disease. This leads to major barriers to accessing these devices in the region. Different regulatory policies and processes adopted across the region make it difficult for manufacturers to navigate multiple regulatory bodies with uneven capacities, resources, and timelines. Weak capacity and misaligned regulatory systems can create a significant delay in the registration of medicines and health technologies.

14 *WHO News.* 2019: Improving Access to Quality Essential Medicines in Kyrgyz Republic. June.
15 WHO HAI. 2015. Medicine Prices, Availability, Affordability in Kyrgyz Republic. *MeTA Project in Kyrgyz Republic.* Bishkek: Medicines Transparency Alliance. https://haiweb.org/wp-content/uploads/2016/10/Kyrgyz Republic-Report-Pricing-Surveys-2015.pdf.
16 E. Mossialos et al. 2016. *Pharmaceutical Policy in China: Challenges and Opportunities for Reform.* Copenhagen: WHO Regional Office for Europe.
17 P. Verhoeven. ABEC Pharma Testing Pre-Feasibility Study. Unpublished (consulted on 25 September 2019).
18 *WHO News.* 2019. Improving Access to Quality Essential Medicines in Kyrgyz Republic. 27 June.
19 Government of Pakistan, Senate Secretariat. 2012. Drug Regulatory Authority of Pakistan Act, 2012. Islamabad. *The Gazette of Pakistan.* http://dra.gov.pk/docs/DRAP%20Act.pdf.

Health Financing

17.   Current health expenditure as a percentage of gross domestic product (GDP) in CAREC countries varies, with Afghanistan spending the highest (9.4%, slightly below the world average of 9.9%) despite being the poorest country in the region, and with Kazakhstan being the lowest (2.9%) (Figure A2.3). High spending on health in Afghanistan is in part related to armed conflict and related foreign aid. Trends in total health expenditure as a percentage of GDP show that most countries have increased or maintained similar levels, over the last decade. Pakistan has maintained a similar level at almost 3%, while Afghanistan has seen small increases since 2009. Azerbaijan, the Kyrgyz Republic, and Tajikistan have shown the strongest growth. Azerbaijan's health expenditure levels almost doubled between 2000 and 2016. The Kyrgyz Republic registered a significant increase, despite decline in the last couple of years.[20] The PRC has seen gradual increases during 2000–2016 (with decline in the years of economic downturn), which has resulted in significant cumulative increases (almost forty-fold over 2 decades).[21] Kazakhstan, Mongolia, and Turkmenistan have witnessed recent decreases in total health expenditure as a percentage of GDP linked to export of natural resources.

Figure A2.3: Current Health Expenditure as Percentage of Gross Domestic Product, 2018

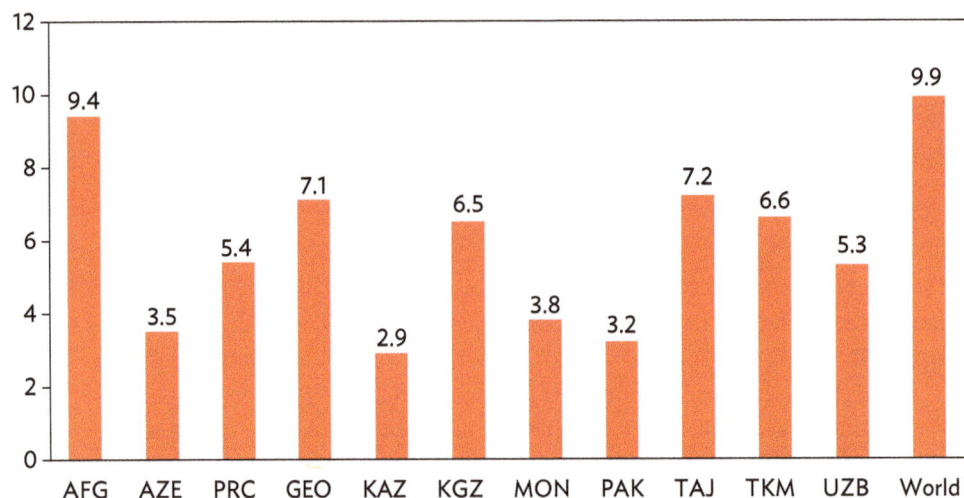

AFG = Afghanistan, AZE = Azerbaijan , GEO = Georgia, KAZ = Kazakhstan, KGZ = Kyrgyz Republic, MON = Mongolia, PAK = Pakistan, PRC = People's Republic of China, TAJ = Tajikistan, TKM = Turkmenistan, UZB = Uzbekistan.
Source: World Bank. World Development Indicators. https://data.worldbank.org/ (accessed 3 April 2021).

---

[20]   Total health expenditure can increase as a result of rising prices in the health sector, increased demand for services, or policies to expand health care coverage. During an economic crisis, countries often aim to reduce health spending in an effort to rein in public budgets. Policies to reduce spending growth include controls on public health worker salaries, halting recruitment and actual reductions in the workforce, cuts in fees payable to health providers, and containment of spending on pharmaceuticals.

[21]   WHO. 2016. *China–WHO Country Cooperation Strategy 2016–2020*. Geneva.

18.   Between 2000 and 2016, all CAREC countries have seen increases in per capita health care spending as well as in out-of-pocket expenditure. Significant increases were seen in Azerbaijan and Turkmenistan, followed by Georgia, Kazakhstan, and Uzbekistan.[22] Globally, there are large differences in out-of-pocket spending by households. Out-of-pocket spending represents 58% of all health spending in the CAREC region compared to 20% in the Organisation for Economic Co-operation and Development (OECD).[23] This compares to 39% out-of-pocket spending on average for LMICs, and 41% for LICs. The average for Central Europe and Asia is at 18% and 65% for South Asia (both Afghanistan and Pakistan included in this region).

19.   As a regressive form of health financing (dependent on the ability to pay), out-of-pocket spending weighs more heavily on poorer households, risking to push them below the poverty line. In countries with a high proportion of out-of-pocket spending, patients are not protected against the financial burden of health care costs. Data on the number of households being pushed below the poverty line is scarce. Figure A2.4 provides an inkling of the kind of effects that high out-of-pocket spending can have on households in CAREC.

20.   CAREC countries are at different stages of introducing national insurance schemes and providing basic health packages. Kazakhstan, the Kyrgyz Republic, Mongolia, and the PRC are scaling up their national health insurance coverage for 80% to 100% of their population. Tajikistan and Uzbekistan are strengthening their national health insurance schemes and defining their basic health care packages. Pakistan has piloted its insurance scheme with in-patient coverage in hospitals, and is currently expanding it to out-patient coverage.

21.   Donor support in the region has been notable in reducing government financial burden by providing access to medicines either for free or at significantly lower costs.[24] Many recipient countries have also benefited from donor-aggregated demand and purchasing mechanisms, negotiated prices, and delivery of commodities. However, some of this support is being withdrawn, which inflicts a triple transition of health care services in CAREC—away from donor aid, a more significant NCD burden, and the funding needs of progressive UHC. These transitions have significant associated costs that will unlikely be met by national resources in the immediate future. As donor support dwindles, countries in the region will be challenged to find ways to obtain quality medicines at affordable prices. This can be done through a variety of mechanisms, such as increasing domestic production, aggregating demand to achieve the benefits that the current pooled purchasing arrangements provide, introducing stronger quality assurance mechanisms for pharmaceuticals, and restructuring procurement systems to increase efficiency.

---

[22] In Azerbaijan, the increase was tenfold, closely followed by a 9.4 times increase in the PRC and 9.3 times increase in Tajikistan. The increases in Georgia (6.4 times), the Kyrgyz Republic (5.9) times, Turkmenistan (5.5 times), Kazakhstan (5.2 times), Mongolia (4.8 times), and Uzbekistan (4.5 times) were more modest but still impressive. Pakistan has seen an increase of 2.5 times, which is significant, given its population size and growth. For Afghanistan, the 2000 figure is not available, but it has seen an increase of 1.4 times since 2009.

[23] OECD. 2018. *Focus on Spending on Health: Latest Trends*. Paris.

[24] Pakistan is the biggest recipient of Gavi, The Vaccine Alliance (GAVI) funds, with $1 billion committed between 2001 and 2019. Donors include GAVI, Global Fund to Fight AIDS, Tuberculosis and Malaria, the World Bank's International Development Association (IDA), the Global Polio Eradication Initiative (GPEI), and the United States President's Emergency Plan for AIDS Relief.

Figure A2.4: Out-of-Pocket Health Care Expenditure in CAREC Countries

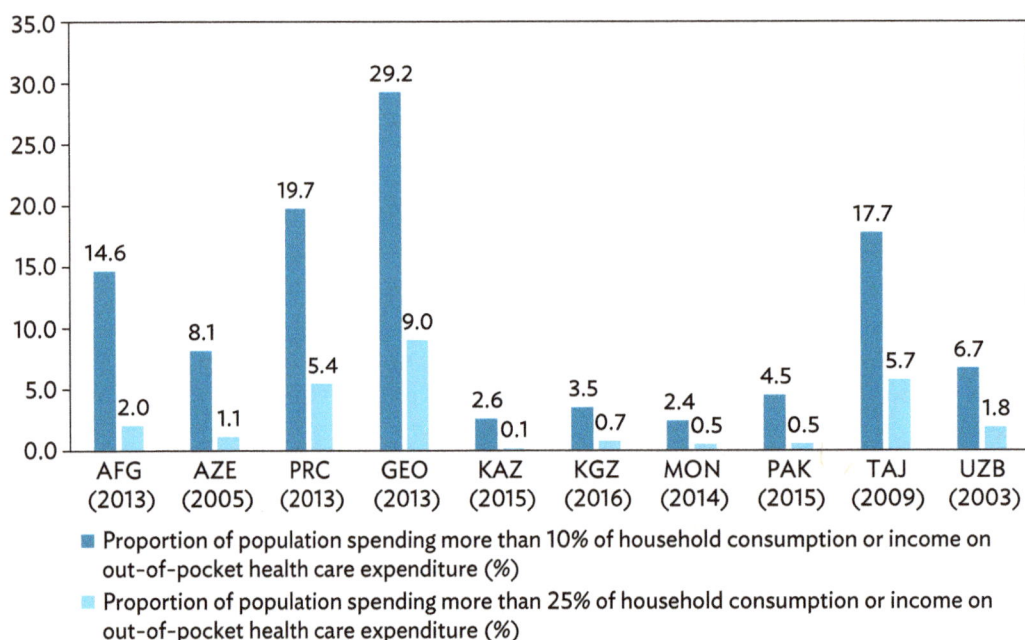

AFG = Afghanistan, AZE = Azerbaijan, CAREC = Central Asia Regional Economic Cooperation, GEO = Georgia, KAZ = Kazakhstan, KGZ = Kyrgyz Republic, MON = Mongolia, PAK = Pakistan, PRC = People's Republic of China, TAJ = Tajikistan, UZB = Uzbekistan.
Note: Data for Turkmenistan are not available.
Source: World Bank. World Development Indicators. https://data.worldbank.org/ (accessed 6 February 2020).

Leadership and Governance

22.	Former Soviet Union republics have demonstrated a strong commitment to the health sector. A variety of health sector models are emerging, ranging from a predominantly public health system like in Turkmenistan and Uzbekistan to a health system based on private practitioners like in Georgia. These health systems are still in transition, such as in terms of public-private mix, health insurance, hospital autonomy, and human resources development. These developments are also increasingly being studied and shared. The PRC and Pakistan have devolved administrations including for health services, which adds a complexity in terms of the federal-provincial relationship and financing of health services. CAREC countries are also strengthening their monitoring information systems to better track their progress toward achieving health results.

23.	CAREC countries also show leadership for health in the international arena. All CAREC governments have regional commitments to health (Appendix 5), and are committed to major international covenants for human rights and equity, Sustainable Development Goals (SDGs), UHC, reproductive health, and climate change. With United Nations (UN) leadership, countries have been invited to align health budgets with SDG commitments. With communicable disease control of WHO and other UN agencies such as the United Nations Children's Fund (UNICEF) and United Nations Population Fund (UNFPA), regional strategies have been prepared for health sector reform and for reforms in subsectors such as IHR, RMNCH, nutrition, control of NCDs, human resources for health, and sector financing.

APPENDIX 3
STRENGTHS, WEAKNESSES, OPPORTUNITIES, AND THREATS ANALYSIS

1.   This section presents the strengths, weaknesses, opportunities, and threats (SWOT) analysis of health sector development and cooperation in the CAREC region (Table A4.1). The SWOT analysis offers suggestions for regional cooperation in health: (i) communicable disease control such as improving laboratories and surveillance, (ii) access to cross-border health services, (iii) quality control of products traded in the region, (iv) improving the quality of care and human resources development, and (v) improving sector policy and financing.

Table A3.1: CAREC Health SWOT Analysis

Strengths	Weaknesses
• Common legacy, regional language • Progress under health MDGs; adoption of SDG-3 and UHC • Established national insurance mechanisms and guaranteed health care packages • Experience in joint or aggregated procurement • Existing health care infrastructure and pool of human resources for health (HRH) • Existing provisions for migrant labor health coverage in national or regional legislation • Significant strengthening of surveillance and response under IHR (2005) • Use of EIDSS to integrate data from different sectors • Existing telemedicine projects addressing health needs of rural populations • Ongoing strengthening of national quality assurance, more laboratories obtaining certification • Capacities for integrated human and animal disease surveillance exist at the central level • Decades of experience in cooperating in other sectors • Linkage to potential projects and investments	• Health sector data availability and reliability • Limited capacity to collect and analyze existing data for improved decision-making • High fragmentation of health surveillance systems (horizontally and vertically) • Lack of intersector coordination between human–animal–plant health sectors • Lack of access to health care for migrant labor • Suboptimal distribution of human resources • Limited government financing • High out-of-pocket payments • High reliance on donor support • Unreliable quality, variable prices of medicines • Lack of regulation around new technologies in health sector, especially around privacy • Weak capacity for human and zoonotic integrated disease surveillance at regional level

continued on next page

Table A3.1 continued

Opportunities	Threats
• Growing cooperation under economic corridors (including in health), such as ABEC and CPEC • National and regional health initiatives, such as GHSA, One Health, Health Silk Road, and APSED III • SPS modernization project in CAREC as well as several other ongoing initiatives that can be built upon • Establishment of regional centers like GDDRC (Kazakhstan), Lugar Center (Georgia), Avian Influenza Collaborating Center (PRC) • Regional training for human resources in health security • Regional health agreements under CIS and SAARC, and recognition of skills of HRH • Growing and dynamic domestic pharmaceutical markets and growing regional demand • Single pharmaceutical market under EAEU • Innovative technology and processes in health • CAREC is well-established, perceived as a neutral and honest broker providing a trusted development platform to support regional development	• New emerging, re-emerging diseases • Withdrawal of donor support • Economic downturns that translate into further reductions of financing for health • Diversity of CAREC countries and proliferation of regional blocs, conflicting agreements • Important regional players (the Russian Federation) that are outside of CAREC but can influence regional policy • Intensified unregulated labor migration • Fragility and conflict • Relative geographical isolation and inaccessible terrain • Relative isolation from international pharmaceutical markets • The complex nature of RCI requires a long period of time to implement • Relatively small size of medical and pharmaceutical markets

ABEC = Almaty–Bishkek Economic Corridor; APSED = Asia Pacific Strategy for Emerging Diseases; CAREC = Central Asia Regional Economic Cooperation; CIS = Commonwealth of Independent States; CPEC = China–Pakistan Economic Corridor; EAEU = Eurasian Economic Union; EIDSS = Electronic Integrated Disease Surveillance System; GDDRC = Global Disease Detection Regional Center; GHSA = Global Health Security Agenda; IHR = International Health Regulations; MDG = Millennium Development Goal; PRC = People's Republic of China; RCI = regional cooperation and integration; SAARC = South Asian Association for Regional Cooperation; SDG = Sustainable Development Goal; SPS = sanitary and phytosanitary; SWOT = strengths, weaknesses, opportunities, and threats; UHC = universal health coverage.

Source: Author's summary based on desk review and discussions with stakeholders.

APPENDIX 4
EXAMPLES OF REGIONAL COOPERATION IN HEALTH

A. Strengthening Regional Health Security

Regional Disease Surveillance Systems Enhancement

1.   The Regional Disease Surveillance Systems Enhancement (REDISSE) project was established under the West African Health Organization (WAHO) of the Economic Community of West African States (ECOWAS).[1] It aims to build national and regional intersector capacities for enhanced collaborative disease surveillance and epidemics preparedness in West Africa by overcoming the weaknesses of the human and animal health systems that hinder efficient surveillance of diseases and response, and in case of emergency, provide immediate and effective response to the said emergency.

2.   The five components of the project include (i) enhancing national surveillance and interoperability; (ii) strengthening laboratory capacity by establishing networks of efficient high quality, accessible public health, veterinary, and private laboratories for the diagnosis of infectious human and animal diseases, and establishing a regional networking platform to improve collaboration for laboratory investigation; (iii) building human capacity and workforce; (iv) enhancing emergency response capacity across the region; and (v) strengthening institutional capacity building, project management, coordination, and advocacy. The project is being implemented as an interdependent series of projects that will eventually engage and support all 15 countries in the ECOWAS region. The project also includes a contingent emergency response component to improve a government's response capacity in the event of an emergency.

Caribbean Public Health Agency

3.   The Caribbean Public Health Agency (CARPHA) conducts regional surveillance of communicable and noncommunicable diseases.[2] It also conducts (i) research on the determinants of communicable disease and on approaches to prevention and control, including cost-benefit studies; (ii) relevant training and capacity building; and (iii) information dissemination in response to outbreaks and to help prevent communicable diseases. It works with national and regional institutions and organizations to (i) coordinate the health response to epidemics and activities on prevention, including immunization; (ii) provide specialized diagnostic and reference laboratory services; and (iii) strengthen

---

[1]   ECOWAS/WAHO. REDISSE Project in West Africa. https://www.wahooas.org/web-ooas/en/projets/redisse-regional-disease-surveillance-systems-enhancement-project-west-africa.

[2]   CARPHA. What We Do. Non-Communicable Diseases. https://www.carpha.org/What-We-Do/NCD/Non-Communicable-Diseases.

national laboratories. It also assists countries in fulfilling the requirements of the International Health Regulations (IHR) (2005).

4.   CARPHA is equipped to investigate and manage communicable diseases, including new and re-emerging diseases, through its network of security laboratories, a variety of specialized units such as an experimental mosquito colony, several epidemiological databases that are maintained within a local area network infrastructure, and an active preventive maintenance unit. The diseases being investigated include vaccine preventable diseases (EPI); HIV/AIDS and sexually transmitted disease; vector borne diseases (dengue fever, malaria, leptospirosis, plague, rabies, and yellow fever); food and water borne diseases (gastroenteritis, diseases caused by salmonella, norovirus, ciguatera, campylobacter, shigella, and E. coli); airborne diseases (influenza-like illnesses, fever and respiratory symptoms, and tuberculosis); and other diseases and syndromes of interest (leprosy, viral hepatitis A and B, meningococcal infection, viral encephalitis and meningitis, and fever and neurological symptoms).

5.   CARPHA is involved in addressing the prevalence of NCDs, which account for the majority of deaths and illnesses in the region. Diseases of concern in the region include hypertension, diabetes, obesity (especially childhood obesity), cardiovascular disease, and cancers such as cervical carcinoma. It focuses on carrying out surveillance of chronic disease and its determinants. This includes behavioral surveillance of risk activities and surveys of such factors as alcohol, drug, and tobacco consumption, diet, adolescent pregnancy, and use of condoms. CARPHA conducts research on the causation of chronic diseases and preventive strategies and health promotion. It is also involved in developing options for preventive action based on scientific evidence, including cost-benefit analyses.

B. Supporting Health Systems Development Through Regional Cooperation

Healthy Ageing Public Procurement of Innovations

6.   The Healthy Ageing Public Procurement of Innovations (HAPPI), supported by the European Commission, is a collaboration of 12 purchasing bodies and innovation experts from eight member states (Austria, Belgium, France, Germany, Italy, Luxembourg, Spain, and the United Kingdom).[3] The consortium aims to identify, assess, and purchase innovative and sustainable health products, services, and solutions intended to improve aging. So far, the partners have developed and purchased more than 150 innovative medical solutions with the help of their procurement strategy. The strategy comprises early market studies and communication of the tender to a multitude of companies including SMEs. The use of functional rather than technical specifications in the tender notices was crucial in this project.[4]

---

[3]   HAPPI Project: Joint Transnational EU Tender. https://ec.europa.eu/eip/ageing/public-procurement-platform/aha-innovative-solutions/5-happi-project-joint-transnational-eu-tenders_en.

[4]   European Commission. 2016. Innovative Public Procurement can Lower Pressure on Health Budgets. *DG Growth: Internal Market, Industry, Entrepreneurship and SMEs.* https://ec.europa.eu/growth/content/8945-innovative-public-procurement-can-lower-pressure-health-budgets_en.

Common Market of the South

7.   The Southern Common Market (MERCOSUR) Multilateral Agreement on Social Security (MASS) was signed as part of regional integration. It has been in force since 2005 in the following signatory nations: Argentina, Brazil, Paraguay, and Uruguay.[5] The MERCOSUR Residency Agreements (RA), promulgated in 2009, incorporated the idea of the MERCOSUR citizen as a person bearing rights, among them, the right to legalization, work, education, and health under the same conditions as nationals of the country in which they reside. The MASS provides the right to social security for persons working in member states and for their family members, ensuring the same rights and obligations as for nationals. In terms of health care, this translates into access to free care through the public health care network in the destination country for temporarily displaced workers and their dependents, if authorized by origin country.

8.   The administrative procedures with regard to health care benefits for workers temporarily domiciled within the territory of another signatory nation, are organized so that the contributions are paid to the competent entity within the host country; however, the other nation's entity provides the coverage. The scope of health care coverage is different in each country. The costs associated with medical care also vary. The host country's managing entity must authorize the granting of health care benefits, and it is the home country entity that will pay for any services that are delivered to the individual. Procedures for reimbursement for certain protracted illnesses are in place, however, their scope and implementation remain imprecise and can hinder timely medical care. The MERCOSUR has established a unified social security database established to facilitate transfer and verification of social security data for individuals within the trade zone. It has considerably reduced the time required to process benefit claims.

9.   In 2003, several South American countries began harmonizing tobacco product taxes to reduce susceptibility to illicit trade. This move also made them less vulnerable to ad hoc agreements with the tobacco industry. These countries also created a common database of the various types of warnings on cigarette packages to support the implementation of the Framework Convention on Tobacco Control (FCTC) at the country level.[6]

Partner Support for Strengthening Domestic Pharmaceutical Industries

10.   Through its Prequalification Program, the World Health Organization (WHO) supports local producers, clinical research organizations, national drug regulatory authorities, and quality control laboratories in achieving the production of quality-assured medicines. This support is provided through (i) training programs (e.g., on good manufacturing practice [GMP], prequalification requirements and bioequivalence); (ii) technical assistance (e.g., provision of expert consultants on GMP, good clinical practice [GCP] or good laboratory practice [GLP], and preparation of regulatory dossiers); and (iii) provision of information and standards. The WHO is also supporting regulatory harmonization efforts in the Southern African Development Community (SADC) and the East African Community (EAC). Similar efforts are also under way within the Economic Community of West African States (ECOWAS).[7] While investment banks, such as the International Finance Corporation (IFC), provide

---

[5]   SciELO. Migration Governance in South America: The Bottom-up Diffusion of the Residence Agreement of MERCOSUR.

[6]   MERCOSUR. 2003. Estrategia Regional para el Control del Tabaco en el Mercosur. CMC/DEC No. 20/03. Montevideo, Uruguay.

[7]   WHO. 2011. *Pharmaceutical Production and Related Technology Transfer*. Geneva.

financing through loans, equity investments or guarantees for viable pharmaceutical production enterprises, such financing projects may incorporate elements of technology transfer. However, the IFC does not have any special programs in place to encourage technology transfer relevant to local pharmaceutical industry development.

Improving Health Services for Migrants and Border Communities

Thailand's Migrant Health Insurance Scheme

11.   Migrants in Thailand are eligible to enroll in either the Social Security Scheme (SSS) managed by the Ministry of Labour or the Migrant Health Insurance Scheme (MHIS) managed by the Health Economics and Health Security Division of the Ministry of Public Health (MOPH). Regular migrant workers employed in the formal sector are able to join the Social Security Scheme with the same entitlements as Thai citizens.[8] Employers and workers each contribute 5% of the worker's salary, and the government contributes an amount equivalent to 2.75%. The MHIS was introduced in 2001, targeting migrant workers from Cambodia, the Lao People's Democratic Republic, and Myanmar.

12.   Those who are not eligible for coverage in other schemes, such as the SSS, must enroll in MHIS. The MHIS is a voluntary prepayment scheme financed by an annual premium paid by the migrant worker (2,200 baht in 2019, equivalent to $73), to receive a comprehensive set of benefits. There is no employer or state contribution, as it is not technically feasible to enforce mandatory participation. The MHIS operates under an annual Cabinet approval document called Measures and Guidelines for Health Exams and Health Insurance for Foreign Workers, through which the extent of coverage of adult dependents is decided on a yearly basis.[9]

13.   The two policy goals of the scheme include screening for and treatment of certain communicable diseases and enabling access to health care for migrants through a defined benefit package. When migrants apply for health insurance, they are required to register at a specific hospital where they go through health screening.[10] The screening includes chest X-ray and sputum confirmation for tuberculosis, and tests for syphilis, microfilaria, malaria, and leprosy, for which a full course of treatment is offered. The benefit package includes comprehensive curative services and a range of prevention and health promotion services, similar to the Thai universal health coverage scheme.

14.   As of November 2018, there are 862,870 migrants enrolled in the MHIS, of whom 91% are migrant workers and 9% are their dependents (footnote 9). According to the Ministry of Labour, the number of insured migrants under SSS has increased from 357,643 in September 2013 to 1,107,426 in September 2018. Given these figures, it can be calculated that approximately 64% of the 3.1 million documented migrants from Cambodia, the Lao People's Democratic Republic, Myanmar, and Viet Nam who are eligible for MHIS or SSS coverage are enrolled. However, there are estimations of an additional 811,437 undocumented migrants who are presumably without health insurance but are technically

8   IOM. *Thailand Migration Report 2019*. Bangkok, Thailand.
9   Government of Thailand, Ministry of Public Health. 2018. One-Stop Service Approaches. Ministry of Public Health, Nonthaburi.
10   Government of Thailand, Ministry of Public Health. 2013. *Measures in Health Screening and Health Insurance for Non-Thai Populations Who Are Not Entitled to the Social Security Scheme*. 13 August. Nonthaburi, Thailand (Referring to the Cabinet Resolution on 15 January 2013).

eligible for coverage under the MHIS. Health insurance coverage for this group of migrants falls to 51% if all eligible migrants (documented and undocumented) are considered.

15.   Before 2013, access to SSS or MHIS depended on whether migrants were legally documented and employed. Undocumented migrants, their dependents, and any documented migrant worker in the formal sector not registered with the SSS were not insured, and faced the possibility of huge payments for health services. Financing for migrant health services was mostly out-of-pocket rather than through a prepaid, pooled mechanism, creating a significant financial burden for service providers. In 2013, the MHIS was expanded to cover all migrant workers not covered by the SSS, regardless of their legal or employment status. As of November 2018, it was reported that, in Thailand, approximately 64% of documented migrant workers from GMS countries who were eligible for health insurance coverage were enrolled. This proportion falls to 51% if all eligible migrants (documented and undocumented) are considered.[11]

[11]   B. Harkins. 2019. *Thailand Migration Report 2019*. Bangkok: United Nations Thematic Working Group on Migration in Thailand. Bangkok.

APPENDIX 5
SUMMARY OF EXISTING REGIONAL COOPERATION IN HEALTH IN THE CAREC REGION

Tables A5.1 and A5.2 show main intergovernmental organizations, other groupings, as well as existing regional initiatives in the CAREC region. Both lists aim to provide an overview and are not exhaustive.

Table A5.1: Summary of Key Health Cooperation Initiatives in the CAREC Region Most Relevant to CAREC Strategy 2030

Approach	Regional Level Interventions	Existing Regional Capacities and Agreements	Examples of Regional Cooperation/Partners Globally
	**Strengthen Regional Health Security**		
Strengthening Regional Health Security (RHS): Introduce early warning and response systems, strengthen intersector coordination (i.e., human, animal and environmental health; border and customs management; agriculture; forestry) and adopt One Health approach at regional level.	• Strengthening of early warning and rapid response mechanisms and harmonization of standards • Strengthening readiness and response capacity for public health emergencies at points of entry • Enhancing cross-border and intersector collaboration under ongoing SPS project in CAREC.	• CAREC SPS standards modernization project	• Greater Mekong Subregion Health Security Project (ADB support) • GHSA • One Health initiative • Belt and Road Silk Health Road • Centers for Disease Control and Prevention (CDC) • World Health Organization (WHO) regional offices
Improving Health Information Systems and Laboratory Networks: Align fragmented surveillance and referral systems, increase capacity of diagnostic laboratories, establish and improve referral systems, introduce common standards, and ensure inter-operability of systems.	• Information sharing • Setting and implementing interoperability standards and disease codification • Establishment of a comprehensive Regional Health Laboratory System	• International Health Regulations implementation • EIDSS • WHO collaborating center on avian influenza (People's Republic of China); Regional Antimicrobial Resistance center (Georgia, Lugar Center); Global Disease Detection Regional Center (GDDRC, Kazakhstan); Biosurveillance Network of the Silk Road (Azerbaijan, Georgia, Kazakhstan, the Kyrgyz Republic, Tajikistan, Turkmenistan, Uzbekistan); Better Labs for Better Lives	• REDISSE • CARPHA • European Union (EU) lab network • CARICOM (CARPHA) • GHSA • One Health • Silk Health Road • CDC • WHO

continued on next page

Table A5.1 *continued*

Approach	Regional Level Interventions	Existing Regional Capacities and Agreements	Examples of Regional Cooperation/Partners Globally
Training and preparation of human resources: Ensure availability of human resources with appropriate mix of skills and competencies.	• Recognition of standards • Joint training and education programs for rare diseases	• FELTP regional epidemiology trainings	• CDC • GHSA • WHO • Private sector
Strengthen Health Systems through Regional Cooperation			
Harmonizing health policies and strategies to enhance noncommunicable disease prevention and control efforts, especially in associated risk factors (e.g., tobacco, alcohol, and food).	• Regional harmonization of tobacco and alcohol taxation • Strengthening tobacco anti-smuggling measures • Regional standardization of food labeling policies	• WHO Framework Convention on Tobacco Control	• MERCOSUR • WHO
Establishing a regional network of surveillance and burden assessment. This network would benefit from cross-country learning. There would also be economies of scale (e.g., from collective bargaining).	• Providing appropriate knowledge solutions for ICT in health • Development and adoption of common data terminology and exchange • Data privacy protection	• Cloud-based service delivery and information analysis, Artificial Intelligence assisted service provision in some countries • Electronic health records, HMIS, and EIDSS	• The International Agency for Research on Cancer (IARC) • European Cancer Information System (ECIS) • RARECAREnet
Establishing a health technology assessment (HTA) institution. Such a body is unsustainable in terms of resources and expertise for a single country, yet the outputs will provide critical guidance on policy development for intervention and treatment.	• Regional procurement of ICT in health after HTA-based recommendations	• China National Health Development Research Center (CNHDRC)	• World Trade Organization (WTO) • International Telecommunication Union • Aga Khan Foundation • ECHO project • NICE • HITAP • Private sector
Collaborating on group purchasing of essential medicines and innovative technologies. Increasing access, affordability, and quality of essential medicines means that the negotiating power of procurement units would expand (especially in smaller countries), and bulk purchasing would reduce costs and help assure adequate supplies.	• Information sharing between national regulatory authorities • Aligning safety and efficacy standards • Conducting joint reviews of research protocols and product dossiers, inspections of research and manufacturing sites • Mutual recognition of assessments and inspections • Strengthening regional quality control and assurance laboratory capacity • Aggregating demand, joint procurement • Increasing domestic production capacity and associated technology transfer • Use of TRIPS flexibilities	• Collaboration under ABEC and CPEC • Existing pooled procurement (GAVI, HOPE, and individual procurement through UNICEF) • Single pharmaceutical market introduced under EAEU • Transfer of technology and increasing domestic pharmaceutical production • Growing and dynamic domestic pharmaceutical markets • Increased regional potential for export (e.g., DAAs for hepatitis)	• EMA • AMRH initiative • BeNeLuxA • EU joint procurement agreement • HAPPI • SADC • PAHO Revolving Fund, OECS, Gulf Council, GAVI, GF, Global Drug Facility, UNICEF • Private sector • BMGF • World Bank • GIPCN • International Finance Corporation • WHO

continued on next page

Table A5.1 *continued*

Approach	Regional Level Interventions	Existing Regional Capacities and Agreements	Examples of Regional Cooperation/Partners Globally
Synergizing regional education and training capacity, adopting innovative technologies to improve education outcomes. Economies of scale from sharing education and training are significant due to existing human resource gaps (skills, people) and migration of health professionals (brain drain).	• Creation of electronic databases connected to employer needs • Harmonization of education standards • Mutual recognition of skills of human resources for health across countries • Telemedicine solutions	• Digital health solutions, such as eLearning and telemedicine projects in Afghanistan, the Kyrgyz Republic, Pakistan, and Tajikistan borders • Provisions under ECIS (the EAEU does not cover mutual recognition of health skills) • Mutual recognition of skills, e.g., CIS	• AFAS • Private sector • International Labour Organization (ILO) • WTO • KfW • Aga Khan • PATRIP Foundation
Improving Health Care for Migrants, Mobile Populations, and Border Communities			
Investing in cross-border service provision to address the lack of and imbalanced geographical distribution of adequate hospital infrastructure, human resources, medicines and technologies, and surveillance.	• Supporting infrastructure development under regional economic corridors and economic zones • Applying GATS to facilitate trade in health (services, people, goods)	• Hospital infrastructure built (CPEC) • Common GOST and SNIPs construction standards remaining from Soviet era • Cross-border telemedicine projects	• Private sector • WTO • ILO
Regional cooperation on provision of health and social benefits for migrant labor. Lack of referral systems for migrants across countries; structural, social, and financial barriers to health and other social benefits that result in faster spread of diseases and higher economic burden.	• Data sharing and establishment of common databases • Connecting migrants to information regarding access to health • Increasing access to health benefits through regional, bilateral, and multilateral agreements and health insurance schemes.	• Provisions existing under EAEU, CIS, and SAARC • Provisions in national legislation covering access to health care for migrants (e.g., Kazakhstan) • Bilateral agreements (limited scope to tuberculosis/HIV) in Kazakhstan, the Kyrgyz Republic, and Tajikistan	• EU • ASEAN • MERCOSUR • GMS migrant labor project • Project HOPE • International Organization for Migration • UNHCR • IFRC • GF

ADB = Asian Development Bank; ABEC = Almaty–Bishkek economic corridor; AFAS = ASEAN framework agreement on services; ASEAN = Association of Southeast Asian Nations; AMRH = African medical regulatory harmonization; BeNeLuxA = pharmaceutical policy initiative; BMGF = Bill and Melinda Gates Foundation; CAREC = Central Asia Regional Economic Cooperation; CARICOM = Caribbean Community; CARPHA = Caribbean Public Health Agency; CIS = Commonwealth of Independent States; CPEC = China–Pakistan economic corridor; DAAs = direct acting antivirals; EAEU = Eurasian Economic Union; HMIS = Health Management Information Systems; GOST = Russian National Building Standards; ECHO = Extension for Community Healthcare Outcomes; EIDSS = Electronic Integrated Disease Surveillance System; EMA = European Medicines Association; FELTP = Field Epidemiology and Laboratory Training Program; GATS = General Agreement on Trade in Services; GAVI = Gavi, the Vaccine Alliance; GDDRC = Global Disease Detection Regional Center; GF = Global Fund to Fight AIDS, Tuberculosis and Malaria; GHSA = Global Health Security Agenda; GIPCN = Global Infection Prevention and Control Network; GMS = Greater Mekong Subregion; HAPPI = Healthy Ageing Public Procurement of Innovations; HITAP = health intervention and technology assessment program; HOPE = Health Oriented Preventive Education; ICT = information and communication technology; IFRC = International Federation of the Red Cross and Red Crescent Societies; MERCOSUR = Mercado Común del Sur (South America common market); NICE = Institute for Health and Care Excellence, OECS = Organisation of Eastern Caribbean States; PAHO = Pan American Health Organization; PATRIP = Pakistan-Afghanistan-Tajikistan Regional Integration Programme; REDISSE = regional disease surveillance enhancement (Africa); SAARC = South Asian Association for Regional Cooperation; SADC = Southern African Development Community; SNIP = Construction Codes and Regulations; SPS = sanitary and phytosanitary standards; TRIPS = Trade-related Aspects of Intellectual Property Rights; UNHCR = United Nations High Commissioner for Refugees; UNICEF = United Nations Children's Fund; WTO = World Trade Organization.

Source: Author.

Table A5.2: Summary of Main Intergovernmental Organizations and Other Regional Groupings Engaged in Regional Health Cooperation in the CAREC Region

Name of the Organization	Members from CAREC Countries	Health Cooperation Focus	Notes	COVID-19 Regional Cooperation Initiatives
Organization of the Black Sea Economic Cooperation (BSEC)	Azerbaijan, Georgia	Focus on (i) elaboration of the Epidemiological Surveillance and Response network within BSEC Member States and establishment of the monthly exchange of information on registered infection diseases between BSEC member states; (ii) exchange of information in case of regional and trans–border emergency situation due to biological agents, including extremely dangerous diseases within the member states; (iii) exchange of information regarding the development of national anti-epidemic, hygiene and sanitary policies and measures regarding sanitary protection of the territories of the member states; (iv) promotion of the internal procedures for signing the Agreement on Cooperation in the Field of Sanitary Protection of the Territories of the Member States of the Organization of the Black Sea Economic Cooperation and exerting efforts to put the Agreement into force; (v) regional cooperation on the implementation of the IHR (2005); (vi) establishing information exchange on preventing counterfeit medicines and the draft of multilateral Memorandum of Understanding on Information Exchange and Cooperation in the Sphere of Quality Assurance of Medicines; (vii) project proposals related to the health care and pharmaceutics presented by the Member States and coordination of development of joint project proposals related to the health care and pharmaceutics; (viii) promoting BSEC–EU cooperation, promotion of the active dialogue with the international organizations, regional cooperation initiatives and programs in the field of health care and pharmaceutics; and (ix) enhancing practical cooperation by participation in the organization of conferences, workshops and seminars initiated by the member states and BSEC Related Bodies, devoted to the issues on the health care and pharmaceutics.	Established June 1992	BSEC has so far focused on addressing negative COVID-19 consequences on the transport sector.[a]

continued on next page

Table A5.2 continued

Name of the Organization	Members from CAREC Countries	Health Cooperation Focus	Notes	COVID-19 Regional Cooperation Initiatives
Commonwealth of Independent States (CIS)	Azerbaijan, Kazakhstan, Kyrgyz Republic, Tajikistan, Uzbekistan	Health Council of the Commonwealth of Independent States focuses on five broad areas of health: (i) quality control of medicines; (ii) medical prevention and health systems development; (iii) epidemiological surveillance; (iv) HIV/AIDS, tuberculosis and malaria; and (v) sanitary security.	CIS Treaty signed December 1991/ CIS Free Trade Area established September 2012	The Russian Federation has made COVID-19 test kits available to other CIS members and access to COVID-19 Russian vaccines is underway.[b]
Cooperation Council of Turkic–Speaking States (Turkic Council)	Azerbaijan, Kazakhstan, Kyrgyz Republic, Tajikistan, Uzbekistan	Focus is on moving toward universal health coverage (UHC), protecting against health emergencies and promoting the well–being of the populations in the Member States of the Turkic Council.	Established October 2009	MOU signed between WHO/Europe and the Turkic Council (11 September 2020). Discussed the European Programme of Work "United Action for Better Health in Europe", that includes potential capacity building activities for protection during health emergencies as well as progress toward UHC such as strengthening data and regulation and ensuring healthy lives for all through vaccination, digital health, and mental health. Antimicrobial resistance and noncommunicable diseases in member states were also discussed.[c]
Eurasian Economic Union (EAEU)	Kazakhstan, Kyrgyz Republic	Focus on: (i) development of health care systems in member countries; (ii) health care and capacity building; (iii) fight against epidemic and/or endemic diseases; (iv) support for maternal, newborn and child health; (v) implementation of international food standards through support, as appropriate, for the Joint FAO/WHO Food Standards Programme; (vi) facilitate cooperation between professional and scientific organizations involved in the development of health care promotion; (vii) facilitate the participation and involvement of civil society in the implementation of health care policy and programs; and (viii) development of a common pharmaceutical market.	EAEU Treaty signed May 2014/ EAEU established January 2015 (preceded by Eurasian Economic Community)	Meeting of the Council of Heads of Authorized Bodies in the Field of Sanitary and Epidemiological Welfare of the Eurasian Economic Union discussed the possible use of "Traveling without COVID–19" information system platform developed by the Eurasian Development Bank.[d]

continued on next page

Table A5.2 continued

Name of the Organization	Members from CAREC Countries	Health Cooperation Focus	Notes	COVID-19 Regional Cooperation Initiatives
Organisation for Islamic Cooperation (OIC)	Afghanistan, Azerbaijan, Kazakhstan, Kyrgyz Republic, Pakistan, Tajikistan, Uzbekistan	OIC Steering Committee for Health's "OIC Strategic Health Programme of Action 2013–2022" focuses on: (i) health system strengthening; (ii) disease prevention and control; (iii) maternal newborn and child health and nutrition; (iv) medicines, vaccines and medical technologies; (v) emergency health response and interventions; and (vi) information, research, education, and advocacy.	Founded in 1969	The OIC Center for Excellence Facilities for Vaccines and Biotechnology products held a series of workshops attended by officials from the National Medicines Regulatory Authorities (NMRAs); Pharmaceutical companies, researchers, and scientists from across the OIC Member States. During the workshop held on 9–10 December 2020 the OIC member states expressed resolve to push for collaboration in the production and distribution of vaccines and medicines. The participants also stressed the importance of effective and timely implementation of two documents adopted by the first meeting of heads of NMRAs from OIC member states the Jakarta Declaration and Plan of Action (Indonesia, 21–22 November 2018).[e]
South Asian Association for Regional Cooperation (SAARC)	Afghanistan, Pakistan,	Focus on: (i) harmonization of animal health legislation and regulation, design and setting up of epidemiological surveillance, disease reporting, and animal health information systems; (ii) regional cooperation in health services (e.g., SATIS); (iii) HIV/AIDS, TB, Malaria; (iv) Tobacco Free Initiative; (v) eHealth platform to enhance infectious disease information exchange.	Founded in December 1985, South Asian Free Trade Area in 2006.	SAARC COVID-19 Emergency Fund was established in March 2020. It was set up to mitigate the negative effects of the pandemic in the region.[f]

continued on next page

Table A5.2 *continued*

Name of the Organization	Members from CAREC Countries	Health Cooperation Focus	Notes	COVID-19 Regional Cooperation Initiatives
Shanghai Cooperation Organization (SCO)	Kazakhstan, Kyrgyz Republic, PRC, Tajikistan, Turkmenistan, Uzbekistan	Within the framework of cooperation the focus is on: (i) construction of medical centers in the core area of the "Silk Road Economic Belt"; (ii) biomedical industry; (iii) traditional medicine; (iv) control of infectious diseases (e.g., The Joint Statement of the Heads of SCO Member States on Joint Response to Epidemic Threats in the SCO Region, 10 June 2018); (v) emergency medical assistance and disaster relief (SCO Mutual Agreement on Disaster Relief); (vi) noncommunicable diseases.	Announced in June 2001; Charter signed in June 2002; Charter entered into force September 2003.	Statement by the Council of Heads of State of the SCO Member States on Joint Response Efforts Against the Novel Coronavirus Infection (COVID-19). (http://eng.sectsco.org/news/20201110/690356.html).[g]

CAREC= Central Asia Regional Economic Cooperation, CIS = Commonwealth of Independent States, COVID-19 = coronavirus disease, EAEU = Eurasian Economic Union, FAO = Food and Agriculture Organization, MOU = memorandum of understanding, PRC = People's Republic of China, TB = tuberculosis, WHO = World Health Organization.

[a] BSEC. COVID-19 Measures for Road Transport in the BSEC Region. http://www.bsec-organization.org/news/1199|covid-19-measures-for-road-transport-in-the-bsec-region.

[b] *Government of the Russian Federation.* 2020. Meeting of CIS Council of Heads of Government. 6 November. Moscow. http://government.ru/en/news/40785/.

[c] WHO. 2020. WHO/Europe and the Turkic Council Begin Putting Memorandum of Understanding Into Action. 3 December. https://www.euro.who.int/en/countries/turkey/news/news/2020/12/whoeurope-and-the-turkic-council-begin-putting-memorandum-of-understanding-into-action.

[d] *Eurasian Economic Commission.* 2020. EAEU Countries' Sanitary Services Manage to Contain Spreading COVID-19. 11 November. http://www.eurasiancommission.org/en/nae/news/Pages/11-11-2020-01.aspx.

[e] OIC. 2020. OIC Member States Reiterate Their Resolve to Collaborate in the Production and Distribution of Vaccines and Medicines. 11 December. https://www.oic-oci.org/topic/?t_id=25026&t_ref=15274&lan=en.

[f] SAARC. COVID-19 Emergency Fund. http://covid19-sdmc.org/covid19-emergency-fund.

[g] SCO. 2020. The Moscow Declaration of the Council of Heads of State of the Shanghai Cooperation Organisation. 10 November. http://eng.sectsco.org/news/20201110/690356.html.

Sources: BSEC. Member States. http://www.bsec-organization.org/member-states; BSEC. Action Plan of BSEC Working Group on Health and Pharmaceutics. (2012–2013). http://www.bsec-organization.org/areas-of-cooperation/healthcare-pharmaceutics/action-plan; CIS. https://cis.minsk.by; EAEU. http://eaeunion.org/?lang=en; OIC. https://www.oic-oci.org/home/?lan=en; Statistical, Economic and Social Research and Training Centre for Islamic Countries (SESRIC). 2013. OIC Strategic Health Programme of Action 2013–2022 (OIC-SHPA). First Draft. Ankara. https://www.oic-oci.org/subweb/ichm/4/en/docs/1_OICSHPA–draft-1-v3.pdf; SAARC. https://www.saarc-sec.org; SAARC. Social Affairs. https://www.saarc-sec.org/index.php/areas-of-cooperation/social-affairs; SCO. News. http://chn.sectsco.org/structure/; SCO. http://eng.sectsco.org/news/; SCO. Statement of the Council of Heads of State of the Shanghai Cooperation Organization on Joint Response to the New Coronary Pneumonia Epidemic. https://www.fmprc.gov.cn/web/zyxw/t1831164.shtml; Turkic Council. Member States. https://www.turkkon.org/en/uye-ulkeler; and Turkic Council. Key Documents. https://www.turkkon.org/en/temel-belgeler.

www.ingramcontent.com/pod-product-compliance
Lightning Source LLC
Chambersburg PA
CBHW050047220326
41599CB00045B/7309